Gender, Genre, and Race in Post-Neo-Slave Narratives

Gender, Genre, and Race in Post-Neo-Slave Narratives

Dana Renee Horton

LEXINGTON BOOKS
Lanham • Boulder • New York • London

Published by Lexington Books
An imprint of The Rowman & Littlefield Publishing Group, Inc.
4501 Forbes Boulevard, Suite 200, Lanham, Maryland 20706
www.rowman.com

86-90 Paul Street, London EC2A 4NE

British Library Cataloguing in Publication Information Available

Library of Congress Cataloging-in-Publication Data

Names: Horton, Dana Renee, 1988– author.
Title: Gender, genre, and race in post-neo-slave narratives / Dana Renee Horton.
Description: Lanham : Lexington Books, [2022] | Includes bibliographical references and index.
Identifiers: LCCN 2022026844 (print) | LCCN 2022026845 (ebook) | ISBN 9781793619136 (cloth) | ISBN 9781793619150 (paper) | ISBN 9781793619143 (ebook)
Subjects: LCSH: Women slaveholders. | Slave narratives. | Sex role. | Slavery in literature. | Slavery in mass media.
Classification: LCC HT871 .H67 2022 (print) | LCC HT871 (ebook) | DDC 306.3/62—dc23/eng/20220714
LC record available at https://lccn.loc.gov/2022026844
LC ebook record available at https://lccn.loc.gov/2022026845

To those who are untragically colored . . .

Contents

Acknowledgments

Acknowledgments are difficult. There are the immediate and apparent acknowledgments (friends and family), but there are also the people who will probably never know how much they influenced me. Recently, I overheard a conversation between a woman and her best friend. She is paralyzed from the waist down and uses a wheelchair. While in line waiting for the concierge to come back from break, I am growing impatient, and she does not seem as if she is paying attention to time at all. She tells her friend that, eventually, her condition will spread throughout her body, and everything will shut down. She says that hopefully, this will not happen anytime soon, and she has to live every day to the fullest because she does not know when her body will shut down. Many of our neighbors greeted her while we were still waiting in line, and her smile never disappeared. As someone who struggles with "time management," it made me realize that I should become more cognizant of how I am spending my time. We hear these cliché phrases about living life to the fullest and seizing the day, but this is one of the few times in my life where I felt a sense of urgency to live. That is when I decided to not wait another month, day, or second to finish this book project. I have something important to say about women slave-owners and post-neo-slave narratives, and it cannot wait. Thank you, my neighbor, for lighting that fire under me.

Now, on to the immediate and apparent acknowledgments . . .

I would like to thank the higher powers and ancestors who are looking out for me.

Thank you, Mom, for being my support system, my shoulder to cry on, and my number one fan.

Thank you to the Temple University, Northeastern University, and Mercy College communities, who were all instrumental in helping me complete this project.

Thank you to all my friends and family for your support and guidance.

Thank you to my childhood and college friends, who never let me forget my working class, Pittsburgh roots. Thanks to: Michael O'Brien, for everything, especially X-Men, the Warhol, and Trolli Eggs; Catharina Lanious, for introducing me to half-marathons and Salem, Massachusetts; Miesha Wiley, for singing along with me whenever "Soldier" by Destiny's Child came on Pandora; Ama Boateng, for your encouraging advice and infectious optimism; and Mayuko Abe, for our great conversations about cultural differences and language acquisitions.

Thank you to Fay and Dennis Greenwald, whose generous support helped me complete this project.

Thank you to Lexington Books and everyone involved in the book manuscript acquisitions, editing, and production process. It was a pleasure working with you.

Introduction

Researching black female slave-owners, and all the nuances that come with such a topic has been a complex experience filled with strange conversations.

I was having dinner with my boyfriend at the time and one of his college friends. My ex's friends were all computer science and technology majors. The few times that I discussed my research with my ex, he never asked questions. In fact, he never had any reactions and did not seem to give two shits about my research. When he attended my conference presentations, he sat in the back and played on his phone, not even attempting to understand my topic. His friend asked me what my research was about, and I said, "female slave-owners." My ex, who never expressed any sort of interest in my research, added, "They're black female slave-owners!" I side-eyed him and sighed. His friend said, "Oh wow. Yeah slavery was interesting. Everyone was in on it. Black women were in on it, too." My glare was still focused on my ex.

Black women were in on it, too. I clarified that black women were a very, very small portion of slave-owners, and although I've conducted archival research about black female slave-owners, most of my research focuses on twenty-first-century representations of female slave-owners. I emphasized that although some black female slave-owners existed, slavery is still a malicious, timeless system that harms everyone involved. At that point, my ex started playing on his phone, his friend was looking out the window, and I realized that this wasn't the conversation they wanted to have.

Black women were in on it, too. Many prominent scholars have already researched how black women are perpetual victims at the bottom of the American social hierarchy. What is missing from these conversations is the idea that some black women in the twenty-first century are perfectly content with this hierarchy, similar to how some women of color, such as Aspasia Cruvellier Mirault, enjoyed the power they gained from slave-owning during antebellum slavery. The narrative that black women only became owners with the noble intentions of freeing their family members does not represent every single case. These are anomalies, but my research is interested in investigating those anomalies, as this is an area of scholarship that has been neglected for far too long.

WHY STUDY FEMALE SLAVE-OWNERS? WHY NOW?

Tire marks, tire marks, finish line with the fire marks/When the relay starts/I'm a runaway slave-master/Shittin' on the past gotta spit it like a pastor

– Iggy Azalea (Amethyst Amelia Kelly), "D.R.U.G.S."

My initial interest in slavery began when I was in fourth grade. I remember my mother's fascination with slavery. She read slave narratives, watched documentaries about slavery, and was curious about our family roots. I didn't appreciate her curiosity until I brought home a chapter on slavery from one of my fourth-grade social studies books. When she read how the chapter likened slavery to indentured servitude and focused on the "positive" aspects of it, she decided that I should start researching slavery with her, and that is when I learned about the trauma and legacy of slavery, as well as how many of the institutions I hoped to study at some day were built by people who looked like me.

Once I entered graduate school, and knew that slavery was much more complicated than what the American grade school system teaches, I became interested in women's role during slavery, as well as in how twenty-first-century artists conceive of women during slavery.

This project started in 2014 with a dissertation proposal. While in graduate school, several personal and political events occurred that shaped my research interests. As I complete this project in 2020, it is imperative that I connect my research to current events. The coronavirus pandemic has swept the world and changed familiar customs, while Black Lives Matter has become more prominent and visible after the death of George Floyd. Now, more than ever, academics must make their research transparent and find ways to connect to the world outside of the Ivory Tower. This project is an attempt to accomplish these tasks.

This project contains artists, writers, filmmakers, and musicians who challenge traditional slavery assumptions, as well as genre conventions. By illuminating female slave-owners and blurring the line between genres, these texts ask us to question our preconceived notions in order to understand not only antebellum slavery, but the twenty-first-century cultural climate as well. Like the texts in this project, my writing style resists the strict boundaries among antebellum slavery, twenty-first-century politics, and my personal research interests by examining the connections among these entities.

The inspiration for this project comes from Iggy Azalea's controversial 2011 song "D.R.U.G.S." where she classifies herself as a "runaway slave-master.[1]" I am interested in how Australian-born Azalea draws upon conventions of slave mastery. Although Iggy Azalea's race is indeterminable, by her own admission, she has advantages in the relay race she raps about in "D.R.U.G.S." due to her positioning in the plantation hierarchy as a white passing woman. She draws upon imagery of antebellum slavery to construct herself as a slave-master. This lyric reads as an attempt to bask in, rather than challenge, hegemonic structures. Many criticized Azalea's lyrics due to the racial connotations, and I am interested in what this line says about the intersection between gender and race, as Azalea is characterizing herself as a skilled white woman slave-master when she crosses the "finish line with the fire marks." "The fire marks" can represent literal fire marks that Azalea leaves when she crosses the finish line—she is so fast that she blazes past everyone—or a reference to the fire marks left on buildings, which were popular during colonial America. In that context, fire marks served as advertisements for insurance companies in addition to signaling that a building was insured. "The fire marks" exemplify Azalea's wealth, as she imagines herself as a slave-master who can afford not only property but insurance and advertisements. The comparison between Azalea's rise in mainstream hip hop and the lyrics' emphasis on white women's role in the slave-owning aspects of slavery demonstrates a temporal shift in representations of slavery in music where women are openly characterizing themselves as metaphorical slave-owners.

In an interview published on *Hip Hop DX*, Azalea apologized for her lyrics and explained that she was sampling a Kendrick Lamar lyric:

> Kendrick Lamar is one of my favorite artists and I loved his song "Look Out for Detox" so much I decided to do my own version of it last year. The lyrics I wrote follow the original version closely . . . The artist's lyric was: "when the relay starts I'm a runway [sic] slave." My lyric was: "when the relay starts I'm a runaway slave . . . Master, shitting on the past gotta spit it like a pastor.

Like many rappers, Azalea takes an intertextual approach to revising this lyric by drawing on representations of plantation dynamics, and she represents herself as a slave-master and Lamar as the slave. When placing Azalea's lyrics in the context of plantation dynamics, as well as twenty-first-century representations of slavery, the ensuing complicated parallel between masculinity and ownership reveals the significance of postmodern techniques.

Azalea's lyrics, as well as the backlash she received, made me interested in twenty-first-century representations of slavery and how those representations may or may not differ from other time periods. What does slavery mean to twenty-first-century artists? How has the current cultural and political climate of the United States changed creative representations of slavery? How has the representation of women evolved, or challenged, previous representations? What is it about our current cultural moment that allows artists to portray black women as slave-owners, an American cultural trope usually associated with white men? Using a black feminist theoretical framework, genre analysis as a methodology, and postmodernism as an aesthetic configuration, my project aims to engage with these questions by examining representations of black and white women slave-owners in twenty-first-century literature, film, music, and art.

Postmodernism and Representations of Slavery

The definition of postmodernism that I utilize in this project comes from Linda Hutcheon, who argues that a foundational characteristic of postmodernism is its ability "to fragment or at least to render unstable the traditional unified identity or subjectivity of character" (90). Identity within a postmodern framework becomes destabilized, and traditional identity categories are fragmented, which challenges essentialist theories about identity. Conventions of postmodernity allow artists to make creative interventions onto the study and representation of slavery. Postmodernism's potential for ingenuity lets artists complicate standard American cultural tropes such as the slave-owner and the plantation mistress. In particular, postmodern conceptions of identity focus on the idea that identity is a performative, rather than fixed, concept, and the boundaries between slave/owner, enslaved/free, and other categories are destabilized. As Brian Ott argues, "How one performs identity has to do with how one conceives of image and reality at/in a particular moment/space," which demonstrates the importance of context and representation in the definition of postmodern identity. Although many of the women in this project seize power in the form of slave-ownership, I argue that they transform into *enslaved* slave-owners where they embody contradictory identity categories.

In addition to the connection between postmodernism and identity, as well as examining postmodernism as an aesthetic, I am also interested in postmodernism as a time period, specifically its relationship to the twenty-first century. In his formulation of the postmodern slave narrative, A. Timothy Spaulding argues "that the discourse of postmodernism played [a] crucial role" in the texts his project examines and focuses on how "the novels were written during the period of time most associated with the rise and development of postmodernism as a theoretical and cultural discourse" (3). For

Spaulding, postmodernism allows for more fantastical representations of slavery, ones that are not limited by realism. I argue that this is what separates the postmodern slave narrative from the neo-slave narrative; as articulated by Bernard Bell and Ashraf H. A. Rushdy, the neo-slave narrative mimics the form of the slave narrative and tries to capture the realistic perspective that made slave narratives believable and marketable. Bell, Rushdy, and Spaulding, in their definitions, focus on representations of slavery in literary texts but do not consider how visual genres interact with and complicate their arguments. Twenty-first-century texts blend multiple genres and modalities, which makes it difficult to separate them into neat categories. Thus, visual, oral, and literary genres in the twenty-first century should be analyzed in conjunction rather than separately.

To address this gap, I propose the creation of a genre that consists of literary and visual texts that exemplify postmodernism's temporal and aesthetic influence on representations of slavery. The definitions of the postmodern slave narrative and neo-slave narrative are preoccupied with the narrative form as a genre, as well as the narrative's relationship to history; while twenty-first-century artists are interested in providing counternarratives, they are also critiquing the popular culture figures that emerged from slavery representations, as several artists in this project discuss the intertextual approach they use to challenge cultural figures in literary and visual texts such as *Gone with the Wind* and *Roots*. Artists of the twenty-first century are utilizing postmodern creative interventions as a strategy for challenging and rewriting American cultural tropes such as the slave, the slave-owner, the plantation mistress, the mammy, and the jezebel.

Post-Neo-Slave Narratives

To reconcile postmodernity, as a temporal, aesthetic, and genre convention, with the neo-slave narrative, I want to employ the term "post-neo-slave narrative." Post-neo-slave narratives are literary and visual texts that mesh conventions of postmodernity with the neo-slave narrative. This subgenre is distinguished from other neo-slave narratives in that these texts apply twenty-first-century theories of identity to the portrayal of slavery. Moreover, unlike neo-slave narratives, post-neo-slave narratives are not limited to literary texts but rather embrace the connections with visual multimedia texts. The texts I include are from the new millennium and were written after Ashraf H. A. Rushdy's seminal book *Neo Slave Narratives: Studies in the Social Logic of a Literary Form*. Similar to how the slave narrative took on an alternative and new meaning during the civil rights era, I argue that conventions of postmodernism have influenced how contemporary writers, filmmakers, and musicians represent slavery in their texts.

My definition simultaneously extends and challenges Margot Crawford's conception of the post-neo-slave narrative. While Crawford treats the post-neo-slave narrative as a "space clearing gesture that shows a conceptual rather than a chronological difference," I am more interested in how the "post" represents both a temporal and aesthetic argument (71). Crawford argues that Amiri Baraka's play *The Slave*, published in 1964, is a post-neo-slave narrative based on its use "of slavery as the frame . . . that encloses the 1960s setting of the play" as well as its implications that "slave narratives and 1960s black nationalism have reached the limits of their ability to explain the real meaning of black freedom and radicalism" (79). *The Slave* sits comfortably in the unknowable and does not attempt to explain what slavery or freedom means. Under my conception of the post-neo-slave narrative, *The Slave* would not count as one, as my project focuses on how artists represent slavery in a twenty-first-century cultural and political climate that stifles, rather than illuminates, identity categories, and Baraka wrote *The Slave* with the context of the civil rights era in mind. My project also extends Crawford's argument of the post-neo-slave narrative as a push "against the time and space of 'slavery to freedom'" by demonstrating how these concepts "can occupy the same temporal and spatial location" (72). Through the examination of the plantation mistress trope, I argue that twenty-first-century artists are demonstrating how women's power was complicated by their status as *enslaved* slave-owners, which shows how they occupied both the free and slave identity categories simultaneously.

The Plantation Mistress in Post-Neo-Slave Narratives

This project focuses on how plantation mistresses are represented in the twenty-first century; specifically, I analyze their construction as enslaved slave-owners who must overcome their subjugation by oppressing others. The post-neo-slave narrative allows for more nuanced portrayals of black women, as "the early twenty-first century . . . is a time when, arguably, there is more space for African American writers to address the lesser-known and more sensitive issues of slavery that complicate the totalizing assumptions of black innocence and white complicity in its evil" (Crawford 76). Postmodern conceptions of identity as fluid and pluralistic make it possible for artists to portray black women as slave-owners, as this is now an identity category that is available to them. Many artists in this project, such as Lalita Tademy and Marlen Suyapa Bodden, problematize the two-dimensional representations of women in depictions of slavery, and they are concerned with the legacy that texts/films such as *Gone with the Wind* and *Uncle Tom's Cabin* has left on American culture.

This project also focuses on plantation mistress's ability to *master* the art of slave-ownership; I used "master" rather than "owner" because I am analyzing the moments where women display their knowledge and mastery of slave-owning as a practice. This is where the conception of a "slave-owning trope" will demonstrate how women act as slave-masters. The slave-owning trope is a term that describes how women slave-owners in post-neo-slave narratives are materially defining their power (or lack thereof). My definition of the slave-owning trope is inspired by the ontological metaphors concept discussed by George Lakoff and Mark Johnson in *Metaphors We Live By*. Ontological metaphors connect "our experiences with physical objects (especially our own bodies) [and] provide the basis for . . . ways of viewing events, activities, emotions, ideas, etc., as entities and substances" (25). Lakoff and Johnson explain how "understanding our experiences in terms of objects and substances allows us to pick out parts of our experience and treat them as discrete entities or substances of a uniform kind. Once we identify our experiences as entities or substances, we can refer to them, categorize them, group them, and quantify them-and, by this means, reason about them" (25). The slave-owning trope gestures toward symbolic registers of slave owning (the master's whip, writing utensils, papers, plantations, tight spaces, chains, etc.) to help the person using it understand their twenty-first-century experiences of the oppressed/oppressor binary. The trope draws a direct link between the past and the present with the user imagining how ownership transforms their present experience into an entity of slavery. The slave-owning trope evokes language that focuses on power, possession, and materiality.

Saidiya Hartman examines the concept of the "afterlife of slavery" in *Lose Your Mother: A Journey along the Atlantic Slave Route*, where she focuses on the racialized violence and racial hierarchal system that still decreases the value of black lives in the twenty-first-century. Twenty-first-century artists depict women as actively participating in oppressing black lives, and thus, keeping slavery afloat. In this book, I will examine how the post-neo-slave narrative connects to the afterlife of slavery, where artists imagine that women participate in racialized violence and keeping racial hierarchal systems intact. Artists depict women as problematically participating in the devaluing of black lives by having them own, rather than free, slaves.

Recently, scholars are re-examining women's complex role in the slave system and challenging the common narrative of how women became slave owners. Traditionally, scholars concluded that women became slave-owners through marriage—women received slaves as wedding presents or were given control of the plantation in their husband's will. In *They Were Her Property: White Women as Slave Owners in the American South*, Stephanie Jones-Rogers discusses the process of girls becoming slave-owners and how young white girls learned how to abuse their slaves by watching their mothers mistreat them (12). Although Christine Walker's *Jamaica Ladies: Female Slaveholders and the Creation of Britain's Atlantic Empire* focuses on female slave-owners in Jamaica during the seventeenth and eighteenth centuries, it details how and why Jamaica had a decent amount of women who owned slaves and arguably became a matriarchal society. Although my project largely focuses on representations of female slave-owners, rather than female slave-owners who actually existed, the complex female slave-owner that exists in post-neo-slave narratives is close to reality, as some black female slaveholders had their children sold away before they became slaveholders, similar to what happens to Caldonia in *The Known World*. I will examine this example even further in chapter 2.

Black Feminist Theory and Slavery

Since black feminist theory is concerned with how women can gain power despite their liminal status, as well as how that power enforces and/or challenges sexual and racial hegemony, it is an appropriate framework for viewing representations of women slave-owners. Black feminist theorists are interested in both the lived experience and fictional representation of black women's lives (see bell hooks, Kimberlé Crenshaw, and Patricia Hill Collins). Deborah White discusses how black women during slavery were placed into two distinct categories: "On the one hand, there was the woman obsessed with matters of the flesh; on the other was the asexual woman. One was carnal, the other maternal. One was at heart a slut, the other was deeply religious" (46). These stereotypes are contemporarily known as the Jezebel and the Mammy, which has real life consequences; Crenshaw describes how black women are considered "more sexual, more earthy, more gratification-oriented. These sexualized images of race intersect with norms of women's sexuality, norms that are used to distinguish good women from bad, the madonna from the whores" (1270–71). The stereotype of black women as angry and overly sexual means that black women, specifically in the United States, are denied the right to be considered victims of rape or domestic violence. As a result, most Americans are less likely to sympathize with black female victims, and black women are less likelier than other groups of women to seek help when they are victims of a crime: "Black women are essentially prepackaged as bad women within cultural narratives about good women who can be raped and bad women who cannot" (Crenshaw 1271).

To relate this back to representations of slavery in American culture, I argue that examining black women slave-owners shifts the narrative from discussions of how black women are oppressed to discussions of how they may have used slave-owning as an attempt to transcend their oppression. Although

White's analysis focuses on slave women, it provides a solid framework for understanding contemporary representations of women slave-owners, specifically how, when considering conventions of postmodernity, the line between slave/slave-owner for women is fluid. In general, White and other black feminist theorists help us understand the multifaceted nature of gender, sexual, and racial inequality and how these inequalities complicate the type of agency that slave-owning women displayed. Although my project focuses on representations of women slave-owners and not literal slave-owners, to provide historical context about slave-owning, it is worth mentioning that legally, women were not allowed to own property in the United States during antebellum slavery, but many of the slave owning women in the texts became owners because their husbands died and left the property to them; thus, ownership is heavily tied to the institution of marriage. Some women in this project used marriage as a strategy for gaining power and increasing their position in the slave hierarchy. Mistress Shaw, a black female slave-owner in *12 Years a Slave*, married the white man who owned her and became the mistress of the plantation that she once worked on. She encourages other black women to take this controversial path and to utilize sexuality as a tool for increasing their position within the plantation hierarchy.

Genre Analysis as Methodology and Practice

This project draws on genre analysis because it allows me to consider the constructive criteria of the post-neo-slave narrative genre. Elizabeth Wardle and Douglas Downs define genres as "types of texts that are recognizable to readers and writers, and that meet the needs of the rhetorical situations in which they function" (Wardle 467). Alireza Bonyadi synthesizes John Swales's, V.K Bhatia's, Maggie Jo St. John's, and Tony Dudley-Evans's definitions of genre analysis into one succinct definition that describes how "central to the analysis of a certain genre is the identification of the moves in a text based on the conventions set by the discourse community. In other words, in genre studies the researcher proceeds with identifying the moves that have been employed by the writers for organizing the information throughout the text" (Bonyadi 87). Genres contain specific recognizable conventions that are distinguishable between different rhetorical situations.

Currently, the neo-slave narrative and postmodern slave narrative are discussed in opposition, and synthesizing these genres into the post-neo-slave narrative allows for a more accurate definition of twenty-first-century texts that considers the interconnectedness of contemporary genres. Scholars have used the term "neo-slave narrative" to describe texts written during and after the civil rights era, and I argue that this term does not encompass the differences between post and pre twenty-first-century texts. Artists in the civil rights era and the twenty-first century are responding to different cultural and political situations in their work. African American writers, such Margaret Walker and Charles Johnson, use the slave narrative as inspiration for their neo-slave narratives, as well as a blueprint for how to fight for civil rights during the 1960s and '70s. Writers draw parallels between the lives of African Americans during slavery and the contemporary injustices black people faced in the United States. Writers mimicked the slave narrative form and wanted their texts to sound similarly to narratives published during slavery. The neo-slave narrative was a replication, rather than an experimentation, of the slave narrative. The twenty-first century saw several groundbreaking events that changed the landscape of the United States—the terrorist attacks of September 11, 2001 and the election of Barack Obama, the first black president of the United States, shifted conversations about identity and civil rights. Since many of the texts I examine in this project were written after these seminal events, I argue that these two events influenced the way writers discussed issues of identity and citizenship. Prior to Obama's presidency, every president was white and male, and Obama's election arguably changed the face of the United States. It was now possible for someone other than a white man to become president of the country, which is something that many Americans did not think would ever happen. The identity category of "president" now becomes available to black people, expanding the possibilities of who can obtain this position. These expanded possibilities changed the way artists depicted slavery in their works—identity categories that seemingly seemed fixed are now destabilized, making it possible for artists to, for example, portray black women as slave-owners. Writers in the twenty-first century are responding to different circumstances than writers during the civil rights era, which is why it is necessary to create a genre the encompasses and illuminates those temporal differences.

A genre analysis approach complements the black feminist theoretical framework this project employs—bell hooks, Deborah White, and many other black feminist scholars are concerned with how a plethora of genres, such as news media, film, and literature, portray black women. Similar to their methodology, I will conduct my textual analysis by looking within and across genres. Post-neo-slave narratives mesh literary and visual texts together and demonstrate the importance of placing seemingly different genres in conversation with each other, as the boundaries between the concepts of "literary" and "visual" are fading during the twenty-first century, especially with the rise of social media. Examining multiple genres allows me to obtain a holistic view of slavery representations.

In addition to utilizing genre analysis as a methodology, this book will challenge traditional academic genres, similar to how other African American scholars incorporate personal experiences into their writing. In her recent biography of Lorraine Hansberry, *Looking* for *Lorraine: The Radiant and Radical Life of Lorraine Hansberry*, Imani Perry describes the book as a "third-person memoir," where she draws parallels between her life and Hansberry's life. Christina Sharpe's *In the Wake: On Blackness and Being* begins with a story about her sister's death. This story aligns Sharpe with the black bodies she analyzes in her text, demonstrating a kinship rather than treating black bodies as distant, inanimate research subjects.

Gender, Genre, and Race in Post-Neo-Slave Narratives is a first-person literary analysis. I am transparent about how my life influences my research interests, and the personal events in my life inform when, why, and how I conducted research on female slave-owners and post-neo-slave narratives. As bell hooks, Patricia Hill Collins, and Geneva Smitherman demonstrate, our personal lives have a tremendous impact on our research, and it is impossible to remove the researcher from the research. I am allowing readers to examine my writing and thought processes with the goal of making academic writing more intriguing and accessible. Similar to the writers in this project, I am interested in challenging the traditional genres we use in academia and making my writing interesting to those outside of the academe. This project experiments with genres similarly to the writers of post-neo-slave narratives. It contains literary analysis, biographies, memoirs, and cultural studies, as a twenty-first-century pastiche of postmodern writing.

There is a tendency in academia to remove ourselves from our writing, or to pretend as if the self does not influence the texts we create and consume. We present our research as if we are omnipresent subjects with no identity. Our identity informs our research, and thus, informs how we present our research. Being more transparent about this will make the research process more accessible and intriguing. My writing style is similar to a new historicism approach, where the events in my life, my preconceived notions about how the world works, and my identity as a black woman shape how I conduct research. On a simplistic level, this explains why two people can read the same text and draw two completely different conclusions—their criticism is based on their academic training, their philosophical views on life, the personal events that shape their interpretations, and so on.

Chapter Overviews

Chapter 1 analyzes the traditional literary version of the plantation mistress trope and focuses on how conventions of postmodernity change the way writers utilize this trope in their texts. I examine these texts through Camilla Dacey-Groth's conception of the "slaveholder narrative" to both reinforce and challenge her definition. While Dacey-Groth encourages white writers to create slaveholder narratives that are reminiscent of ones created by Thomas Jefferson, I argue that Valerie Martin's *Property* and Marlen Suyapa Bodden's *The Wedding Gift* focus more on creating post-neo-slaveholder perspectives that complicate the traditional definition of the slaveholder narrative. I argue that through conventions of postmodernity, both writers create white women slaveholders whose identity function between competing binaries and who explicitly imagine themselves as slaves despite their status as owners. Although Martin is a white woman, Bodden is an African American woman who initially wrote *The Wedding Gift* from Sarah's perspective because she wanted to "give voice to [her] ancestors who were kidnapped from Africa during the transatlantic slave trade" (308). She then added Theodora's perspective because she realized that their stories were so intertwined that Sarah's story did not make sense without Theodora's. Theodora is the white female-owner of the plantation where Sarah is enslaved. Toward the end of the text, Sarah utilizes slave-owning tactics to seek revenge against her husband and father, which, I argue, challenges the traditional representations of slave women in slave narratives and neo-slave narratives, making *The Wedding Gift* a post-neo-slave narrative.

Chapter 2 continues the conversation about traditional representations of the plantation mistress by examining how race complicates this trope. Many black female slaves in *Cane River* and *The Known World* reinforce rather than dismantle the institution of slavery, and slave-owning is a method they use to distinguish themselves from black slaves. Audre Lorde's famous quotation provides a crucial framework for understanding these texts: "The master's tools will never dismantle the master's house." Several case studies in this project demonstrate that to become a slave-owner and inherit property, a woman has to become a mistress or wife first; however, Doralise Derbanne in *Cane River* challenges this rule, as she is born a slave, freed by her white slave-owning father at the age of two, and becomes a slave-owner while she is still a child. Caldonia in *The Known World* becomes a slave-owner when her husband, Henry, dies, and has trouble maintaining order of the plantation. In particular, the slaves do not treat Caldonia with the same amount of respect as they treated Henry. Caldonia embarks on a sexual relationship with Moses, one of her slaves, and he is the first slave that her late husband purchased. I argue that Caldonia's characterization is similar to that of the white male slave-owner who rapes and abuses his slaves, as she uses her relationship with Moses to gain intel on the other slaves and does not genuinely love him. This controversial characterization of a black woman exemplifies the creative possibilities that postmodernity provides—Caldonia's relationship with Moses flips power dynamics between black women and black men.

Chapter 3 focuses on fictional representations of plantation mistresses in film with an emphasis on Mistress Epps and Mistress Shaw from *12 Years a Slave* and Lara and Broomhilda from *Django Unchained*. I argue that both films are post-neo-slave narratives due to their postmodern treatment of slavery—both films utilize fantastical and supernatural elements in their representations of slavery, specifically as a method for reimagining slavery's monstrosities. My analysis focuses on the moments where *Django Unchained*, which scholars typically read as playful and exaggerated, engages in realistic portrayals of slavery and *12 Years a Slave*, which scholars praise for its historical realism, uses elements of fantasy when deviating from the original narrative. These moments involve women—in *Django Unchained*, Lara is characterized as a skilled slave-owner and madam while Broomhilda is treated as the damsel in distress, which is striking because black women are usually not portrayed as damsels; in *12 Years a Slave*, Mistress Shaw and Patsey are more prominent characters in the film than they were in the original narrative, which I attribute to the increase of activism by black feminists who demand that filmmakers provide more complex representations of black women. I argue that both films utilize a slavery framework to provide commentary about the current American cultural climate by drawing subtle connections between contemporary America and antebellum slavery.

Chapter 4 analyzes music by Missy Elliott and Rah Digga, two black women rappers who were popular at the turn of the century. I argue that in Digga's "Harriet Thugman" and Elliott's "Work It," both rappers use slave-owning metaphors and characteristics to craft their identities. Both rappers use two famous examples of rebellious slaves (Kunta Kinte and Harriet Tubman) to signal their hip hop identity as powerful women. My analysis focuses on the persona that Missy Elliott and Rah Digga put forth in their work and not their identity outside of the context of their music. In their lyrics, they emphasize their influence and power over others by drawing attention to their lyricism. In "Harriet Thugman," Rah Digga raps: "Do away cats with the same ol' wack/Lead a nation up north where the real party at" (Rah Digga 2000). She shows how she owns them lyrically when she does "away" with them and subsequently gets to decide who comes "up north where the real party at" with her. Similar to Rah Digga, Elliott also emphasizes her lyrical prowess when she raps that "When I come out you won't even matter," which shows how she lyrically owns other musicians to the point that their presence is moot (Missy Elliott 2002). Throughout both songs, Digga and Elliott shift between the slave/owner and enslaved/free binaries to imagine the slave-owning methods black women might have utilized to gain power, freedom, and agency.

I conclude with a brief analysis of Kara Walker's representations of slavery in silhouette form. In this section, I read Kara Walker's work as a post-neo-slave narrative due to her nuanced representations of women. My analysis focuses on the slight positions of power that Walker places slave women in, where she makes us questions the identity of the silhouettes. Much of my analysis focuses on "Untitled 18," a silhouette from Walker's "Emancipation Approximation" series, where the slave woman and the plantation mistress are intertwined, making it difficult to neatly determine which is the slave and which is the owner, as well as what race each woman is. I relate this back to conceptions of postmodern identity where seemingly competing subject positions are present within the same woman. Similarly to other artists within this project, Walker's work challenges the binaries between slave/owner and enslaved/free.

Project Goals: Introducing Transparency in Academia

The purpose of this project is to provide an alternative understanding of slavery representations in the twenty-first century, one that places women at the forefront of the scholarly conversation about slavery. As identity categories, "slaves" and "slave-owners" are still strongly associated with men, and my project aims to complicate the masculine and racial connotations of these categories. I intend to blur the boundaries between literary and visual texts; in the twenty-first century, the strict conventions associated with these genres are rapidly disappearing, and the intertextual aspects of the post-neo-slave narrative places the visual and the literary within the same genre category.

I will also provide new language and criteria for evaluating representations of slavery in the twenty-first century. Scholars, such as Stephanie Li, have likened many texts in this project to neo-slave narratives, which, I argue, is an insufficient framework to describe these texts as neo-slave narratives were created during a specific cultural moment (the civil rights era). As a result, civil rights era artists used the slave narrative differently than twenty-first-century artists with some scholars, such as Salamishah Tillet and Dacey-Groth, arguing that we are living in the post-civil rights era. The neo-slave narrative functions as a memetic genre that places slavery in its historical context with little deviation from the original conception of slave narratives. The texts in this project do not attempt to replicate slave narratives and are more interested in using conventions of postmodernity such as sampling, intertextuality, and character fluidity to blur the boundaries between different genres and identity categories.

My project aims to provide new language for discussing representations of black women in American slavery based on their innovative characterizations in these texts. Black women were usually not characterized as slave-owners, colonizers, and damsels in distress, and artists are drawing on these cultural tropes in ways that challenge the traditional conceptions of them. The goal of my project is not to diminish the real discrimination that black women face but to analyze how postmodernity allows for more complex representations of black women that demonstrate the ways that they replicate, rather than challenge, hegemonic structures.

My project seeks to answer the following questions. First, how has the twenty-first-century cultural climate changed slavery representations? Similarly to the neo-slave-narrative being influenced by the civil rights era, how has the post-9/11 era affected slavery representations? The neo-slave narrative emerged during the civil rights era, when black authors drew upon the slave narrative as inspiration for their contemporary fight for equality. Books such as Sherley Anne William's *Dessa Rose* and Charles Johnson's *Middle Passage* mimicked the style and language of the slave narrative and drew comparisons between the civil right era and transatlantic slavery. Our current cultural and political climate in the twenty-first century is different than the civil rights era—authors are not mimicking the slave narrative genre the way the neo-slave narrative did and are more interested in complicating, rather than replicating, the slave narrative genre. Since my main argument is that the post-neo-slave narrative describes the texts in my project more accurately than other terms, answering this question will demonstrate the importance of creating a new category and providing new language for these representations.

The next question my project seeks to answer is: How has identity as pluralistic and fluid changed the way women, particularly black women, are portrayed as colonizers and owners? Because the post-neo-slave narrative focuses on postmodern identity and is less concerned about providing an accurate portrayal of slavery, representations of women are different than they were in slave narratives and neo-slave narratives. In the other two genres, authors were hesitant to portray black women as agents of the slave system who happily kept the slave economy afloat. This allows for more interesting and complex representations of black women and challenges the idea that black women during slavery can only be portrayed as helpless victims.

Through this project, I want to align academia with the larger public. Due to the rise of Black Lives Matter and other social justice movements, academia should produce scholarship that is readily accessible to the larger public. I am not asking for academics to "dumb down" their work but rather to become more transparent about their research interests and to write in more interesting prose that refrains from tedious, impenetrable jargon. I am part of my research on female slave-owners. The stories I tell throughout the text are part of the research narrative, as this project has consumed the last eight years of my life. I am transparent about how my textual interpretations are shaped by my Temple University and Northeastern University education, my poor upbringing in Pittsburgh, my curiosity about the way black women can gain power in a system that is seemingly not built for them, and my understanding that academia is not necessarily receptive to a voice like mine. With this book, I hope that more academics will utilize transparency when presenting their research, which can help bridge the gap between the ivory tower and those outside it.

NOTES

1. Although she spent most of her childhood in Australia, she moved to the United States as a teenager and settled in Atlanta, Georgia. She was previously signed to rapper T.I.'s Grand Hustle Records. Azalea raps with an exaggerated Southern American accent that many critics chastise her for. Several hip hop artists, including Azealia Banks, Q-Tip, and Eve, accused Azalea of being an inauthentic and terrible rapper who appropriates black culture. In particular, rappers felt that Azalea performs an exaggerated black female stereotype persona.

Chapter 1

The Female Slaveholder Narrative

Challenging the Plantation Mistress Trope in Property and The Wedding Gift

In the *Washington Post* article, "Can Black Women and White Women Be True Friends?" Kim McLarin analyzes the complicated relationship between Missy Anne and Kizzy in the film version of *Roots*. Missy Anne asks Kizzy, " . . . don't you want to be my slave? Aren't you my friend?" "Friend" and "slave" are intertwined, and in order for Kizzy to become Missy Anne's friend, she has to become her slave. This framework provides the basis for the contemporary mistrust between black and white women, where black women are expected to nurture and coddle white women, which is reminiscent of black women's role during antebellum slavery. McLarin recalls experiences where white women threw the strong Black woman stereotype onto her and denied her vulnerability and humanity, similar to how Missy Anne treats Kizzy.

Antebellum slavery left a traumatic legacy that still impacts people, of all races, in contemporary culture, and one of those legacies is the complicated relationship between black and white women. Because black women were forced to obey white women by taking care of their children, laboring in the fields, and tending to the kitchen, genuine friendships, where both parties are on equal footing, were difficult. Solidarity among black and white women, both literarily and historically, was complicated by intersecting issues of identity, race, and class. Carby questions the "strands of contemporary feminist historiography and literary criticism which seek to establish the existence of an American sisterhood between black and white women" by examining the many failed political and personal alliances among these groups (6). Although there are literary and historical examples to support

Carby's assessment, this chapter is interested in exploring how white female slave-owners, and the black women they own, occupy competing binaries. These relationships are illuminated in post-neo-slave narratives.

The post-neo-slave narrative is a genre that embraces ambiguities and complexities. Rather than finding a solid answer, the post-neo-slave narrative treats identity as both/and instead of either/or. This concept of identity is illuminated in Valerie Martin's *Property* and Marlen Suyapa Bodden's *The Wedding Gift*, as both texts demonstrate how white female slave-owners occupied competing binaries—oppressed/oppressor, slave/slave-owner, and powerful/powerless. As Toni Morrison notes in her dust cover praise, *Property* captures the complex interiority of a white female slave-owner who attempts to navigate a slave system that oppresses her, yet allows her to live a relatively comfortable life.

This chapter will analyze literary representations of the methods women use to gain power within a hierarchy that places them below white men, including the use of slave-owning as a path toward citizenship and legibility, and I will critique the financial and physical materials that are associated with slave-owning. Valerie Martin's novel *Property* and Marlen Suyapa Bodden's novel *The Wedding Gift* illuminate the perspective of white women slave-owners who gained power through the subjugation of slaves. Martin and Bodden portray white women slave-owners as occupying competing binaries—they are oppressed/oppressor, slave/slave-owner, and powerful/powerless simultaneously—which characterizes them as *enslaved* slave-owners. While *Property* is a first-person narrative told from Manon Gaudet's perspective, *The Wedding Gift* focuses on two perspectives: Theodora Allen, a white woman slave-owner who is abused by her husband and disappointed that her daughter is not a proper southern belle, and Sarah, a black woman slave who utilizes slave-owning tactics to kill her slave-owning father, sell her cheating husband back into slavery, and free her family and herself from slavery. These representations of women during slavery focus on how their performances of power interact with their victimization, which aligns with postmodern conceptions of identity as pluralistic and fluid.

In the twenty-first century, although representations of women as slave-owners in literature and popular culture have increased, white men are still the default face of slave-ownership. In *Women and Slavery, Vol 2.: The Modern Atlantic*, Claire Robertson and Marsha Robinson challenge the notion that "Women, slave and free [are] assumed to be universal victims and lack agency" and encourage scholars to explore women's complex role during American slavery (274). While they acknowledge that women were indeed oppressed and did not legally have as much power as men, they also show that women's status as victims, regardless of race, during American slavery is complicated by the various ways they displayed agency. Similar to the claims that Robertson and Robinson make, in "*Ar'n't I a Woman*, Gender, and Slavery," Leslie Harris discusses the legacy of Deborah White's book *Ar'n't I a Woman: Female Slaves in the Plantation South* and argues that, with the exception of White's book, the general American narrative of slavery depicts slave-owners and slaves as men with an emphasis on how men are emasculated or hypermasculinized. Harris describes how:

> Most historical works on slavery had already created a vision of the slave family as dysfunctional and . . . of slave men as "emasculated": deprived of their proper roles as heads of households by paternalistic masters; rendered permanent 'boys' by white owners; unable to protect their wives and children from physical, emotional, and sexual incursions by masters and overseers (*mistresses rarely, if ever, figured in these discussions*); and limited in their ability to engage emotionally with children or lovers. (150; my emphasis)

Harris's analysis focuses on how the structure of slave culture emasculates male slaves while simultaneously highlighting how historians rarely discuss the ways in which mistresses participated in that emasculation. She emphasizes how both the oppressors and oppressed during slavery are often gendered male—the power that white slave mistresses wielded and the experiences of black slave women are subsequently diminished. American culture is still hesitant to confront issues of slavery, let alone the idea that women slave-owners existed. American representations of powerful women in slave culture do not focus on their slave-owning practices. Although some scholarship has emerged about representations of women's slave-owning practices, the sources I highlight all point to the lack of attention paid by scholars to both fictional and literal representations of women's role as slave-owners (black and white) during antebellum slavery.

To illuminate black women's experiences during slavery, in "Reflections on the Black Woman's Role in the Community of Slaves," Angela Davis outlines the various methods that female slaves used to rebel against the institution of slavery, including poisoning their masters' food and setting plantations on fire. Davis briefly comments on how black women worked toward purchasing their family members' freedom, which, in some ways, is acting as a slave-owner. The power dynamics between the slave-owning class and the slaves they own are different; slaves did not set up the economic structure that they had to work within to free their family members. However, they are still buying into the idea that people can be bought in the first place. Exploring this complex dynamic of slave-owning can help expand our understanding of what constitutes slave-owning and how black female slave-owners, even with benevolent intentions, were still enforcing the slave system. Throughout Davis's essay, she calls for more historical research on black women's complex role during slavery, and analyzing black women's role as mistresses answers Davis's call.

WOMEN, SLAVERY, AND ECONOMIC
POWER/MASTERY

This chapter explores how twenty-first-century writers engage with the concept of "slaveholder narratives," which Camilla Dacey-Groth describes as narratives that tell the story of slavery from the perspective of the oppressor as well as "literature by white authors on white Americans' experiences of slavery" whose purpose is to bridge "the black-white gap in understandings of slavery and its legacy" (152–53). Dacey-Groth argues that the relative absence of slaveholder narratives by American authors represents "white America's past inability or unwillingness to engage in *Vergangenheitsaufarbeitung*, a German term coined to refer to the monumental task of dealing with the past of the Holocaust . . . " (153).[1] The slaveholder narrative was a prominent genre in the eighteenth and nineteenth century with writers such as Thomas Jefferson (*The Writings of Thomas Jefferson* and *Notes on the State of Virginia* [1853]), Thomas B. Chapin (who wrote several diary entries about slavery in 1845), and William Byrd (*The Secret Diary of William Byrd of Westover, 1709–1712*) reflecting on their slave-owning experiences. Some slaveholder narratives featured tight records of which slaves were whipped, sold, or ran away, such as Byrd's, while others, such as Jefferson's, grappled with the moral and political ramifications of owning slaves. Like the renewed interest in slave narratives that happened during the 1960s and 1970s, Dacey-Groth is arguing for the emergence of a *neo*-slaveholder narrative where, like the original conception of the slaveholder narrative, white authors reflect on the historical and contemporary impact slave holding practices had on the United States. This relates to her argument that reparations to African Americans is a fiscal and moral obligation, and she argues that white American authors can help other white Americans understand that reparations are a necessity by demonstrating how slavery informs contemporary hegemonic structures.

Although Dacey-Groth's text was published in 2009, twenty-first-century American authors, I argue, are attempting to understand slavery's legacy by re-imagining both the neo-slave narrative as well as the plantation mistress trope through postmodern conventions such as intertextuality, contradictory identity categories, and dismantling strict binaries. By meshing postmodern conventions with the slaveholder narrative, Valerie Martin's *Property* and Marlen Suyapa Bodden's *The Wedding Gift* complicate this concept by demonstrating ways in which white women slave-owners act as both oppressed and oppressor simultaneously. I argue that the slaveholder narrative is constructed differently in the twenty-first century due to postmodernism's influence on identity categories. What characteristics does the slaveholder narrative contain when placed in a twenty-first-century American context where "colorblindness" is celebrated? Through the exploration of women's complex roles during slavery, I argue that Martin and Bodden align contemporary America with its slavery roots by demonstrating how the present is informed by the past.

In addition to illuminating the voices and perspectives of slaveholders, both texts also complicate the plantation mistress trope, typified by Scarlett O'Hara in *Gone with the Wind*, by demonstrating how women participated in the economic exchange of slaves—though Scarlett interacts with her slaves, she is never depicted as selling slaves or determining which slaves should or should not stay on the plantation. However, Manon (*Property*) and Theodora (*The Wedding Gift*), the main characters in each novel, are consistently represented as being intimately involved in the economics of the institution—including purchasing slaves and ensuring the continuing economic success of the plantation—while simultaneously acting as benevolent slave-owners. I argue that this characterization of women slave-owners as skilled participants in the slave economy is made possible by conventions of the post-neo-slave narrative—since identity is constructed as fluid in the twenty-first century, contemporary writers have more power to depict women as oppressors, which results in a strong implication of women slave-owners for their role in slavery that differs from previous representations where women were not chastised for keeping the slave economy alive. Thus, the post-neo-slave narrative challenges traditional representations of both slavery and women to show how women's role during slavery went beyond the common characterization of them as powerless victims.

Representations of Slavery in American Literature

The civil rights era, which focuses on the 1960s-1970s, saw a renewed interest in slave narratives as well as black rights activists who drew parallels between contemporary forms of discrimination against people of color and the treatment black people received during slavery. This is where the slave narrative received renewed interest and occupied a similar purpose as it did during slavery. The neo-slave narrative emerged, and Bernard Bell provides the criteria for this new genre when discussing *Jubilee*: "Margaret Walker gives us our first major neoslave narrative: residually oral, modern narratives of escape from bondage to freedom" (289). Ashraf H. A. Rushdy's definition is more specific and focuses on the first-person persona captured in neo-slave narratives. This first-person voice speaks to the witnessing and testifying that occurred in first-person antebellum slave narratives; as in, the narrator was given more credibility if s/he could tell his or her own story. Rushdy argues that while neo-slave narratives contain a certain amount of nostalgia, "there is also a critical examination of those issues, movements, and outcomes of the sixties" (5). Thus, not only did the neo-slave narrative critique slavery but it also made a political statement about black inequality in the 1960s and '70s, simultaneously making a historic and contemporary argument for civil rights.

I argue that we are currently in the post-civil rights era and as a result, texts written during this era, even ones about slavery, differ from its civil rights era counterparts. The texts that I examine in this chapter, as well as in the rest of the project, were written after Rushdy's seminal book *Neo Slave Narratives: Studies in the Social Logic of a Literary Form* and require new language and criteria to examine them. A significant difference between the civil rights era and the post-civil rights era is the language Americans use to discuss race as well as the construction of identity. Modernist theories of identity purport that it is a fixed, stable category that allows no flexibility. This led to theories of essentialism that insisted on inherent racial differences that people are born with. However, identity is constructed differently in the post-civil rights era and is considered fluid and destabilized. In their examination of national identity, Bradatan, Popan, and Menton argue that identity fluctuates based on the social situation: "Defining social identity as a fluid rather than rigid characteristic brings up the idea of a fluctuating national identity depending on the contexts and relationships with other social actors. Different contexts require different sets of actions and behaviors and the one who knows both sets of rules well can feel comfortable and can function well in various situations" (transnationality as a fluid social identity). This characterization of identity as fluid and depending on context is a key feature of post-neo-slave narratives and represents a departure from the neo-slave narrative. In neo-slave narratives, slaves journey from bondage to freedom and do not partake in the slave economy. In post-neo-slave narratives, women slave-owners are both free and bonded simultaneously, and the story does not focus on their oppression, which is why twenty-first-century authors are more willing to implicate women for their role in slavery and depict them as agents of the slave system—our current cultural moment allows for such nuanced characterizations.

THE PLANTATION MISTRESS IN LITERATURE

Although Scarlett O'Hara is the quintessential plantation mistress, her characterization is based on other plantation mistresses that came before her. The plantation mistress trope is featured in several eighteenth- and nineteenth-century novels and slave narratives, including Harriet Wilson's *Our Nig: Sketches from the Life of a Free Black, in a Two-Story White House, North*

(1859) and Harriet Jacobs's *Incidents in the Life of a Slave Girl* (1861). Mrs. Bellmont, the antagonist of *Our Nig*, is abusive toward Frado, the protagonist of the narrative, and acts more vindictive toward her than the white men in the house. Mrs. Bellmont overworks Frodo and whips her for petty reasons. Frado characterizes Mrs. Bellmont a "she-devil" who is "wholly imbued with southern principles," suggesting that Mrs. Bellmont's evilness is built into the fabric of southern culture. In *Incidents in the Life of a Slave Girl*, when Jacobs's grandmother is being sold at the slave auction, she is bought by an older woman, her grandmother's deceased mistress, for fifty dollars. Mrs. Flint, Jacobs's owner at that time in the narrative, is described as "deficient in energy" but having "nerves so strong, that she could sit in her easy chair and see a woman whipped, till the blood trickled from every stroke of the lash" (12). While Mrs. Flint was supposed to be a kind, Christian woman, she still participated in slave culture and did very little to stop it. The plantation mistress trope is a focal point of southern plantation culture as well as a case study for how to understand the hierarchy and nuances of antebellum slavery.

The goal of Catherine Clinton's *The Plantation Mistress: Woman's World in the Old South* was to rewrite the plantation mistress trope; specifically, Clinton wanted to "focus on a character both overlaid by romantic mythologizing and considerably shortchanged by traditional literature" (Clinton xi). Clinton's exploration of the plantation mistress trope was one of the first to focus on the power and agency that white women held during slavery. Clinton recognizes how in the master class, "sons received land and daughters, slaves" and thus, white women were slave-owners who could inherit property from their families (37). She also emphasizes how the "total control of reproductive females was of paramount concern for elite males" (6). Since the publication of her text, several scholars have challenged Clinton's study and her emphasis on white women. In *Reconstructing Womanhood: The Emergence of the Afro-American Novelist*, Hazel Carby challenges the argument that Catherine Clinton puts forth in *The Plantation Mistress* about women's reproductive value in slave culture by considering how black women's reproductive value differed from white women's: "As a slave, the black woman was in an entirely different relation to the plantation patriarch. Her reproductive destiny was bound to capital accumulation" (24–25). Thus, while white women were producing future American citizens, black women were producing capital, and although Clinton briefly mentions white women's slave-owning practices, Carby stresses the significance of white female slave-owners who owned capital and kept the institution of slavery thriving. Carby problematizes Clinton's study by examining the intersecting oppression black female slaves faced:

In Clinton's historical analysis of the plantation mistress, she argues that white slave-owners used "similar methods of keeping blacks and women excluded from spheres of power . . . and employed near-identical ideological warfare against them." But if women, as an undifferentiated group, are compared to blacks, or slaves, as an undifferentiated group, then it becomes impossible to see the articulations of racism within ideologies of gender and of gender within ideologies of racism (25).

The foundation of Clinton's study assumes that black slaves are not women and women are not black slaves, which diminishes black women's experiences. Carby emphasizes that this foundation does not allow for a fruitful comparison of black and white women's slavery experiences.

After exposing the limitations of Clinton's study, *Reconstructing Womanhood: The Emergence of the Afro-American Novelist* focuses on the binaries that constructed black womanhood and white womanhood. Black womanhood and white womanhood had competing criteria and features: "Strength and ability to bear fatigue, argued to be so distasteful a presence in a white woman, were positive features to be emphasized in the promotion and selling of a black female field hand at a slave auction" (25). Black women were valued for their work production while white women were valued for their purity and delicacy. Contemporary representations of slave culture continue to construct black and white women using these binaries that emerged during slavery. As a result, black women field slaves are constructed as work horses and white plantation mistresses are constructed as dainty. However, *Property* and *The Wedding Gift* challenge this static representation by constructing both white women and black women as *dainty work horses*, a contradictory characterization that demonstrates how Martin and Bodden are using conventions of postmodern identity to deconstruct original conceptions of women's role during slavery.

The most famous representation of a plantation mistress in American culture is Scarlett O'Hara, the main character in Margaret Mitchell's *Gone with the Wind*, which Leah Rawls Atkins argues relies heavily on the plantation mistress stereotype of white women as "weak and fainting" (93). O'Hara is treated as if she is a delicate flower by the other characters, and her character speaks to Clinton's assertion that the plantation mistress trope suffers from romantic mythologizing. Bell also refers to *Gone with the Wind* as "romantic nostalgia" since it is dissimilar to narratives that are concerned with the grittiness of slavery such as Margaret Walker's *Jubilee* (289). In *Gone with the Wind*, Mitchell uses the plantation mistress trope to camouflage the grittiness of slavery by characterizing white women as meek and using them as aesthetic props. However, *Property* and *The Wedding Gift* feature more complex representations of white women in nineteenth-century American slave culture. In both novels, white women are active participants in many aspects of slave culture, but at the same time, their power is limited due to their gender. They struggle to conquer the plantation hierarchy where men were regarded as the head of the household even when there was no man around. In *Property*, even though Manon's husband dies, leaving her in control of the plantation, it is his former presence, not Manon's physicality, that still runs the plantation and dictates what goes one.

The idea that slaveholding is a masculine task is one that appears in several other American novels. Toni Morrison's *Beloved* questions the concept of benevolent slave-owners as well as whether or not women can become successful owners. Mrs. Garner, the white female slave owner who takes possession of Sethe and the other slaves after her husband dies is not outwardly vindictive to Sethe the way Mrs. Bellmont is to Frado and even provides Sethe with gifts and affection. However, scholars have discussed how Mrs. Garner's benevolent slave-owning is just as dangerous as villainous owners. Nancy Jesser argues that Mrs. Garner " . . . cannot conceive of life at Sweet Home without a white master" and she invites School Teacher to take over the plantation (343). I want to emphasize that Mrs. Garner cannot conceive of a life at Sweet Home without a white *male* master. This is important to highlight because it suggests that for Mrs. Garner, slave owning is a masculine task that women are too weak to handle. The plantation mistress, then, becomes one who cannot become a successful owner who masters the economic aspects of slave owning. This characterization is one that both *Property* and *The Wedding Gift* deconstruct.

The White Woman Slave-Owner in Neo-Slave Narratives

The white woman slave-owner is a figure that appears in neo-slave narratives such as Charles Johnson's *Oxherding Tale* and Sherley Anne Williams's *Dessa Rose*. Flo Hatfield in *Oxherding Tale* is portrayed as sexually deviant and mischievous. She is different from the usual white male plantation owner that is portrayed in American literature, and while she participates in the sexual exploitation of black male slaves, she is also characterized as having drug addiction, which portrays her as both a victim and an oppressor. In addition to her sexual behavior, she has been married many times, which is not common for women during this time, and most women stayed widowed after their first husband died or did not remarry if their husbands left. A drug addicted, sexually free, and complex slave-owner is perhaps the direct antithesis to more traditional representations of slave-ownership, as Flo features characteristics of both "benevolent" and violent slave-owners.

In *Dessa Rose*, Ruth Elizabeth (Rufel) is portrayed as Dessa's savior after Dessa is taken to her plantation after being rescued from a lynching. Rufel participates in a scheme to purchase slaves, free them, and then use the money to escape her own dire circumstances. Dessa and Rufel develop a friendship that confuses themselves as well as those around them, and Rufel goes so far as to nurse Dessa's baby. This raises the question of genuine friendship between slaves and slave-owners. Can they become genuine friends in an antebellum slavery context where white women slave-owners have more power over black women slaves? The concept of friendship across race and class lines during antebellum slavery appears in both *The Wedding Gift* and *Property* with both texts concluding that such arrangements are inherently beneficial to the slave-owner due to the power she wields.

Female Slaves as Wedding Gifts

The story of slavery is told from the perspective of the white woman slave-holder, which, I argue, is Martin's and Bodden's attempts to disrupt the masculine discourse surrounding this topic. *Property* and *The Wedding Gift* both critique the practice of giving slaves to women as wedding gifts and complicate the idea of wedding gifts as intimate and humane. This challenges romance genre conventions where wedding gifts symbolize happiness and hope. In order for women to receive property, they themselves must become property by getting married, which epitomizes the concept of women slave-owners are commodities who commodify slaves. Both novels also challenge the idea that genuine friendships can exist between a slave and the owner. I also argue that friendships across racial and class lines could not genuinely exist in these representations of slavery because of inequality—both Theodora and Manon think that their friendships with Sarah (the name of the slave woman is the same in both texts), who they own, are meaningful, but it is clear that the friendship is actually one-sided—the slave-owner is the one who benefits from it financially and emotionally. Although these two texts are popular and have received many awards, little academic scholarship exists about them, which makes them the ideal case studies for this chapter.

Property is the story of Manon Gaudet's loveless marriage and dissatisfaction with life as a plantation owner in Southern Louisiana in 1828. Although she owns property, including many slaves, she utilizes material language to construct herself as a piece of property who is part of the material plantation culture. When Manon's aunt tells her that she is concerned about her not being able to conceive children, Manon describes herself as "not a marriageable commodity," which demonstrates how she recognizes her positioning in plantation culture. Although she is a slave-owner, she is also a commodity, and she is now a tainted commodity because she is older, widowed, and cannot have children. Creole Louisiana is an ambiguous cultural space consisting of American, French, and Spanish cultures. Slave-owning within this region functioned differently than other parts of the United States, which Lalita

Tademy's *Cane River* illuminates as well. Slave-owners within this region kept meticulous notes on their slaves and other property, which was usually not the case in other American regions during this time period. This meticulous record keeping is what makes Manon shatter the image she had of her father being an honorable, hard-working man. Louisiana also had a robust free people of color population, and they often had their own thriving areas where they had slaves of their own. Manon is disgusted, yet intrigued, by free people of color, especially after learning that her crush, Joel, frequents neighborhoods of color.

Manon also visualizes herself as a slave when she looks at her father's portrait and feels her head bursting, as if "an iron collar" similar to one "used to discipline field women [was] fastened on [her] skull" (182). The "iron collar" is a material entity of slavery that symbolizes docility and pain, and chains are an object that appear frequently in slave narratives. Manon imagines that she is being disciplined similarly to field slave women, which exemplifies how she views herself as a slave—not just a slave, but a field slave who is at the bottom of the plantation hierarchy. She imagines that her husband is "turning the screw of the hot iron collar tighter and tighter until my skill must crack from the pressure," which shows how she fantasizes about dying similarly to how slaves were killed. Some slaves also, as a form of resistance, committed suicide rather than deal with the inhumane treatment they received during slavery, and Manon evokes thoughts of suicide in this scene. This scene demonstrates the material aspects of Manon's enslavement and ownership—she is, contradictorily, both the owner and the slave on this Louisiana plantation.

Manon models her slave-owning identity after her father, and that crumbles throughout the text when she begins to unravel her father's hypocrisy. As a child, Manon thought that her father died during a slave insurrection, as her mother and family did not tell her the truth. After his death, Manon comes across two black boys at the edge of a dock, and one gloat that " . . . your pappy set that fire hisself and shot himself in the head, so he dead already when the beam came down on him" (47). Initially, Manon sees her father as a strong slave-owner who provided for his family, and wants to use similar slave-owning tactics as him. She builds an image in her head of her father as a hero, and she does not want to believe that he committed suicide and left her family to fend for themselves. Manon's fantasy begins to crumble after her mother dies and she reads her father's journal, where she noticed that he never wrote about her, upset because she thought she would "figure in his life more importantly than his hoe or sick field hand, which, after all, received a mention in his journal" (182). Manon's concludes that her father was obsessed with his slaves, as well as his slave-owner identity, and she adopts this persona by being obsessed with Sarah.

Manon learns how to be a plantation mistress through Sarah, even though Sarah is her slave and wedding gift. In response to one of her husband's many outbursts, Manon "looked at him blankly, without comment, as if he was speaking a foreign language" (8). She confesses that this is a trick she "learned from Sarah," and it "unnerves" her husband (8). Manon treats her husband as the "other" whose actions and words are incomprehensible, likening him to something foreign and indistinguishable. Sarah gains power and control through silence and pretending as if she does not understand what others are doing and saying, and Manon utilizes this strategy as a way to unnerve her husband, embodying the familiar idea that silence speaks volumes.

Manon's ambiguous identity extends to her treatment of black women. Throughout the text, she is simultaneously envies, admires, and admonishes black women. She is disturbed when she learns that her crush, Joel, hangs out in the free people of color section of the town and enjoys the company of multiracial women. Manon describes one of the "light-skinned courtesans" (161) she encountered at Mrs. Perot's house as follows:

> What struck me most about the horrible creature was her excellent French. That perfect accent coming out of that yellow face, those dark eyes flashing with rage, made her seem like a grotesque doll, created as some sort of poor joke, which I suppose is exactly what she was, what they all are. (162)

Like her father, Manon is repulsed and fascinated by black people, as she uses competing language to describe the light-skinned courtesan. She describes her as a "horrible creature" with "excellent French," as well as a "grotesque doll." In post-neo-slave narratives, identity is fluid, with one person occupying multiple categories, no matter how contradictory they may seem. Manon demonstrates this through her contradictory description of this unnamed woman, as she is both attracted to her and disgusted by her. She attempts to dehumanize the woman by calling her a "creature" but still noticed her "excellent French."

Manon functions as the man and slave-owner to Joel's woman and suitor. Joel primarily seeks a woman with money, and he entertains Manon as long as she is wealthy. After Manon's husband dies, she realizes that he was heavily in debt due to his poor plantation management, which makes her an inadequate suitor for gold digging Joel. This flips plantation customs during that time, as Manon is the one who acts as the male suitor to Joel's feminine passivity, and Manon is the one who has to prove her financial stability to gain Joel's affection. This, coupled with her inability to have children, makes Manon a failure in both male and female roles. Her inability to conceive means that her money is the most important thing she can offer a partner, and she sadly realized that "It was money, only money, that would keep Joel from ever being more than my friendly admirer" (148), which is illuminated by Joel giving her a "brotherly kiss on each cheek" before leaving her house (150).

When Sarah is captured after running away from the plantation, Manon learns that she passed up north as a white man, which causes her to tell her aunt that Sarah "has tasted a freedom you and I will never know" and has "traveled about the country as a free white man" (189). Manon's remark focuses on Sarah's mobility—she is able to travel and leave the plantation. The plantation becomes an insular setting where no one, except white men, are free, and Manon is envious that Sarah experienced freedom. Thus, Manon characterizes herself as a slave because she cannot leave the domestic sphere, and she views Sarah as having more power and autonomy than her. Manon is careful to say Sarah has tasted "a freedom" rather than "freedom" or "the freedom," which is a slight recognition of the small amount of power she does wield on the plantation. Manon is free, but she is not free in that way that an autonomous white man is. Although she recognizes her power, she still feels that the freedom Sarah had was the quintessential example of living without bondage.

Before Manon's husband dies, she fantasizes about controlling the financial aspects of the plantation, and she pities her husband for being an inadequate owner. She imagines

> selling them all and the house and the land, settling his debts, which are considerable. He has loans from his brother and three banks, and he has used the house as collateral for repairs on the mill. He has what my father called "planters disease"; he keeps buying land when he hasn't the means to cultivate it. If the price of sugar falls again this year, it will hurt him, but he won't have the same sense to stop planting to meet the shortfall. He doesn't know I can read an account book, but I can, and I've been looking into his for some time now. He might pull through this year if the weather is good and the price stable, but this combination is unlikely, as good weather means a better crop for everyone, which will drive the price down. I never speak to him about such things. (16)

This passage exemplifies Manon's construction as both a financially fluent slave-owner as well as an enslaved wife. When Manon suggests that she is not allowed to read an account book, she appropriates the reading trope, which is a common feature in slave narratives. Slaves were forbidden to read and write, and it was illegal for anyone to teach them how to. Thus, her husband treats her like a slave and keeps her in the dark about the financial aspects of the plantation. Despite her characterization as a slave, she demonstrates fluency in financial matters when she provides concrete details for how her husband can pay his debts and get the plantation to run smoothly. Manon's knowledge of plantation owning comes from her father, and since he has discussed financial issues, it sounds as if her father is grooming her to become a plantation owner, not merely a wife. She cannot speak with her husband about these issues because as a woman on a plantation, she does not have the right to discuss financial problems, which circles back to her characterization as a powerless slave.

Manon places herself in the position of the slave and imagines ways that they use space as a form of empowerment. One night, when Manon looks outside of her window, she sees a "negro, dressed in a white shirt and loose breeches that whipped around in the wind" at the foot an oak tree (31). The slave's clothing becomes a material representation of whipping, and Manon imagines that his breeches are whipping the slave, as if the slave is whipping himself. She then describes how she "couldn't make out his features" and asks if he was "one of ours" (31). The act of turning the slave into a faceless entity allows Manon to treat the slave as a blank canvas. This act of defamiliarization allows Manon to place herself in the slave's position later in the text. After breakfast, she begins wondering around the area where she saw the slave:

> I was thinking about the man . . . I walked out to the oak where I had seen him and looked among the roots for any shoe prints or anything he might have dropped, but there was nothing. I stood exactly where he had stood and looked up at the house. I could see my bedroom window—one curtain was fluttering half outside in the breeze—and my husband's window as well. When I looked at the kitchen yard I could see right into the top of the mill and the dirt road running to the quarter. Quite an excellent command post. (43)

Manon puts herself in the slave's position when she "stood exactly where he stood," which exemplifies her attempts to think of herself as a slave. Since Manon feels that the domestic space is oppressive and restrictive, she imagines that the area outside of the home is free. She describes this space as an "excellent command post" and sees it as an area of power and control. In this passage, the slave transforms from being disempowered to being an omniscient presence who can observe everything that goes on in the plantation, and for Manon, this is a desirable position within the plantation hierarchy.

Contrarily, while Manon is fascinated by the power she perceives slaves to have, she characterizes Sarah as the proper plantation mistress. While Manon is standing in front of the oak tree, imagining herself as a slave, she sees Sarah standing in her bedroom, holding a baby. She describes how Sarah "just stood there, her dress half-opened, looking at me coolly." Since Manon is infertile, other characters see her as flawed since women during this time were expected to have children, especially since her husband has fathered many children with slave women. The image of Sarah in the bedroom with a half-opened dress and a baby represents sexual objectivity and fertility. Sarah looks at Manon "coolly," as if she is not afraid of her and expects Manon to see her desirability. Her ability to have children contributes to her desirability since she can provide Manon's husband with property. This is a reversal of many scenes in texts about slavery—the plantation mistress is usually the one who observes the plantation from the top of the house, representing her statute and power. However, Sarah is the one in the position of the mistress, suggesting she has a certain amount of power that Manon does not have access to due to her infertility. This scene also demonstrates that Manon sees being a male slave as a more powerful position than her current predicament; as Manon imagines herself as a male slave, she now has the freedom to view Sarah as a sexual object, as this is not something she can do as a plantation mistress.

The book ends with Sarah's safe return to Manon's plantation, and Manon confronts Sarah for running away and leaving her to die after the insurrection. "When you gets to the North," Sarah teases, "they invites you to the dining room, and they asks you to sit at the table. Then they offers you a cup of tea, and they asks, 'Does you want cream and sugar?'" (192). The table is a common metaphor in African American literature. In Langston Hughes's "I, Too," Hughes says "Tomorrow/I'll be at the table/When company comes," which demonstrates the importance of having a proper seat at the table and not being banished to other areas of the house. The goal of Audre Lorde's *Kitchen Table: Women of Color Press* was to empower women of color and demonstrate that their voices belonged at the head of the table. Sarah emphasizes the equality she felt up North after being invited to sit at the table. Manon imagines a "colorless Yankee woman" serving Sarah tea and the "righteous husband" getting a cushion to make Sarah more comfortable. This "perfectly ridiculous" image exemplifies Manon's lack of mobility and inability to understand a world outside of her own, one where Sarah could have a seat at the table. Manon treats Sarah as both her runaway lover and runaway slave, angry that Sarah did not consider "whom she left behind" when she escaped up North (192).

Manon characterizes herself as immobile because she cannot leave the domestic sphere and envies slaves like Sarah who are not stuck on the plantation. In her mind, the mobile slave is higher within the plantation hierarchy than the plantation mistress. In *The Wedding Gift*, a similar dynamic occurs where Sarah is able to dictate from afar what happens on the plantation she escapes from, and she holds more power as an escaped slave than she did when she lived in the domestic sphere. While Manon never escapes her enslavement, Sarah becomes a free woman who travels beyond American borders, and the plantation becomes a space that enslaves *everyone* regardless of race and gender identity.

Enslaved Slave-Owners in *The Wedding Gift*

Marlen Suyapa Bodden's *The Wedding Gift* is told from two perspectives—
Theodora Allen, who is Cornelius Allen's wife and the mistress of the
Alabama plantation, and Sarah, Cornelius's slave daughter who is given to
Clarissa as a wedding gift, making Sarah Clarissa's sister and slave. While
Theodora's chapters focus on her loveless marriage and indifference toward
slavery, Sarah is planning an escape from the Allen plantation after her sister
is brutally raped by overseers. Theodora is dissatisfied with life as a plantation mistress and aspires to be a writer and artist. She wishes to become a
full-time writer without dealing with her plantation mistress duties. The irony
of this is that Theodora already has plenty of time to create her writing and
artwork because most domestic plantation duties are handled by slaves. When
Theodora tells her father that she wants to become a writer, he "laughed," and
insisted that "Gentlemen do not find lady novelists feminine" while encouraging her to "keep a journal that [he] shall read" (65). Theodora learns that
her aspirations are not aligned with her plantation mistress duties, as well as
her father's conception of white womanhood. Although journaling is typically a private form of communication, a relationship between the self and
the journal medium, Theodora's father insisting that her private thoughts are
for public consumption takes away Theodora's agency, as well as limits the
genres of writing she can use, as writing novels isn't "feminine."

Unlike Manon, Theodora is characterized as naïve and usually avoids discussing slave owning practices. She is surprised to learn that other plantation
mistresses take on a more active role in the financial aspects of slavery. When
discussing house slaves with Emily, her sister-in-law, Theodora is baffled by
Emily's insistence that she chooses their house servants at the slave auction
"and never the pretty ones" (124). Emily problematically suggests that there
is a correlation between a slave woman's attractiveness and a slave-owner's
willingness to rape her. This idea supports the stereotype that white plantation
mistresses are shallow, petty, and only care about the aesthetic aspects of the
domestic sphere. Theodora tells Emily that she is not allowed to choose her
own slaves, and she describes herself as having a "melancholic mood," suggesting that the inability to make financial decisions saddens her. Theodora
accepts the institution of slavery and barely questions its presence or her role
within it. She asks Emily to join her at the party downstairs because "there
really was nothing to say about matters over which [they] had no authority"
(124). Theodora accepts her role as a plantation mistress with very little resistance, and she, very easily, dismisses her own dreams and aspirations in favor
of keeping the plantation system afloat.

Theodora is a surprisingly flat character with not much character development, although this may relate to Bodden's original conception of this novel.

The Wedding Gift was initially supposed to focus on Sarah's journey from bondage to freedom, similar to other narratives about slavery, but Bodden decided to add Theodora's perspective because she wanted to challenge herself and see if she could write from a white female slave-owner perspective (307). The meshing of these two viewpoints transforms the text from a standard slave narrative to a post-neo-slave narrative where a multitude of slavery perspectives live within one text. With this new configuration, *The Wedding Gift* is no longer a text that focuses on one singular slave experience but demonstrates the complex nature of slavery, providing several counternarratives that challenge the traditional American narrative.

While Theodora provides the plantation mistress perspective, I am interested in the moments where Sarah uses slave-owning tactics as a strategy for power and control. The novel ends with Sarah's shocking confession—after she discovers that her light-skinned husband and first cousin, Isaac, was cheating on her with Clarissa, her sister and owner, she plots revenge against him. She describes how she sold Isaac back into slavery as well as how she murdered her father and former slave-owner:

> I encouraged Isaac to flee and wrote him a paper that he thought was a traveling pass. That pass instead instructed anyone who read it to take Isaac to Allen Estates for a reward of $200. My heinous acts did not end there. To prevent him from finalizing a document that revoked the promised freedom for my mother, Belle, Bessie, Dottie, and Eddie, and to avenge his sale of Belle to the Reynolds plantation, I killed Cornelius Allen, by mixing small poisonous amounts of bloodroot in his drinks. (304)

The quest for knowledge, as well as the journey to learn how to read and write, is a popular trope in slave narratives. This literacy, however, is normally used as a method of subversion, and slaves use literacy as a tool for helping to plot revenge against their masters. However, Bodden flips this trope by demonstrating how literacy is used against other slaves. When Sarah adapts the tactics used by slave-owners to sell her husband back into slavery, she re-construes power dynamics between fellow slaves. She takes advantage of Isaac's illiteracy similar to other slave-owners and banishes the idea that slaves felt a sense of camaraderie among themselves, which is a common theme in slavery representations. Though Sarah was not strictly forbidden to mix herbs and chemicals together, her mother, Belle, taught her how to mix a few poisonous drinks and made her promise that she would not tell anyone about these recipes. This exemplifies another instance of Sarah using knowledge and literacy to demolish the plantation hierarchy, and she snatches power away from her father by using her skills as a chemist to overthrow him. She feels detachment from her father, which is why she calls him

"Cornelius Allen" rather than "my father." However, it was this familial bond that allowed her access to the plantation house. The domestic space becomes a place of power and subversion for Sarah—being within close proximity to her owners allowed her access to the food, poison, ink, and papers that she needed to successfully free her family. She ultimately flips the script on her father and husband, literally and figuratively, by changing what the documents say.

Sarah's confession presents her as both a slave and slave-owner, which is a crucial characteristic of postmodern identity and something that differs from non-twenty-first-century representations of slave culture. Postmodern identity claims that identity categories are destabilized, and within this area of destabilization is where opportunities for power and subversion occur. After Sarah's confession, she addresses the audience and asks for their mercy:

> Reader, I ask that you do not judge me harshly and that you view my deeds not through the prism of your time but through that of mine. It is true that what I did was evil, but I can see that only now. Then, I was a child who did not know the fortitude that I possessed. Now that I am no longer chattel, I know that a slave does not have to be like his master, and that retribution does not belong to any of us, but to the Lord. (304–5)

This passage demonstrates the postmodern technique where writers deconstruct the idea that time is static, and the present becomes a tool that writers use to read the past and vice versa. Sarah becomes a time traveler whose character exists in both the twenty-first century and during antebellum slavery. She places retribution in a religious context and suggests that those who seek it are acting as if they are the Lord. There is a sense of immortality that lingers underneath the surface of this passage—Sarah received a glimpse of what it is like to play God when she successfully sought revenge against her husband and father as well as likened herself to a slave-owner—and she can speak to twenty-first-century audiences because she is not inhibited by time and space constraints.

The passage also relates to an interview that Bodden conducts with Bookreporter.com, where she encourages readers to use antebellum slavery as a catalyst for fighting against contemporary forms of inequality. Bodden tells readers that she wants "them to say, 'I enjoyed that story.' Then, I want them to think about modern human rights violations, that there are at least 27 million slaves around the world *today*!" (312). She puts antebellum slavery in a global conversation about human rights, inequality, and slavery in the twenty-first century. Essentially, Bodden argues that past human rights violations will help readers understand present ones, similar to how civil rights activists used the slave narrative as a historical document that helped them understand inequality during the sixties and seventies. Where Bodden's text differs from representations of slavery during that time period is, like other writers in this project, she constructs black women as colonizers who utilize slaveholding tactics against other slaves in order to further their position in the plantation hierarchy. This characterization of black women is realized by conventions of postmodern identity where contradicting subject positions are championed—black women are thus constructed as both slaves and owners, challenging the idea that black women are only represented as slaves who fight against the plantation system.

CONCLUSION: THE IMPORTANT
OF COUNTERNARRATIVES

Property and *The Wedding Gift* grapple with the material resonances of slavery, untangling the gift giving practices of slave-owners during this period. Black women slaves become gifts that white women use for both companionship and work. Although Clarissa and Manon attempt to become friends with their slaves, the power dynamics of slavery make it impossible for these relationships to function as anything other than exploitive and uneven. The practice of giving slaves to recently married women as wedding gifts highlights how women's path toward citizenship and legibility is connected to their ability to become slave-owners, as slave-owning was a method they could utilize to become important members of the planter class. *The Wedding Gift* highlights the subversive tactics Sarah uses to free herself and her family, and she is able to seize freedom more easily than the white female slave-owners. Although Sarah was Clarissa's wedding gift, throughout the text, Clarissa's aptitude for slave-owning diminishes while Sarah's increases, which flips the dynamics between slave and slave-owner; their father wants Clarissa, his white daughter, to transform into a skilled slave-owner, but it is actually Sarah, his slave daughter, that masters slave-owning practices.

Both texts portray women's role in the postmodern conception of the South by providing counternarratives that challenge narratives of slavery portrayed in texts such as *Uncle Tom's Cabin* and *Gone with the Wind*, and the narrative of plantation mistresses as weak and naïve, typified by Scarlett O'Hara, is destabilized. Similarly, the next chapter will continue to focus on intertextuality and counternarratives, as *Cane River* and *The Known World* both seek to rewrite popular representations of slavery in American literature. The post-neo-slave narrative illuminates postmodernism's emphasis on plurality and fluidity, as its goal is to demonstrate that characters are not forced to choose between competing subject positions as well as highlight the importance of showing multiple perspectives on slavery, including ones that challenge traditional representations of the plantation mistress.

NOTES

1. Although Dacey-Groth argues that white Americans are currently not writing slaveholder narratives, they did exist past the nineteenth century. Thomas Dixon's *The Leopard's Spots: A Romance of the White Man's Burden 1865–1900*, published in 1902, is the antithesis of *Uncle Tom's Cabin* and portrays white Southerners as heroes.

Chapter 2

"Sometimes, One Must Become a Master to Avoid Becoming a Slave"

Cane River, The Known World, *and the Postmodern Black Plantation Mistress*

"I assume you will write about black female slave-owners fondly," a friend said, after accusing me of participating in "mesearch."

"Mesearch" is the pejorative term[1] used to describe "autoethnography," which is when researchers examine their personal experiences in conjunction with the social and cultural research they conduct. I argue that every researcher participates in mesearch—researchers bring their identity and schooling to their studies. As Victor Ray notes in the *Inside Higher Ed* article, "The Unbearable Whiteness of Mesearch," "White norms and culture are projected as universal standards," and because whiteness is considered default, these claims are often not leveled at white scholars. I approach the study of female slave-owners through the lens of my upbringing and identity as a black woman, just as scholars from other backgrounds bring their identity to the text. Rather than ignore our personal experiences, researchers should make these experiences transparent and visible to their audiences; research interests start with the self, with ideas formed by our various identities and backgrounds, and to pretend that this is not the case, or that only scholars of color do this, is inaccurate and false. Our research interests, and the mediums we use to explore our ideas, do not occur in a vacuum. Black feminist scholars, such as bell hooks, Patricia Hill Collins, and Michele Wallace, ask us to examine how our identities influence the research we conduct, the way interviewees react to us, and the spaces we are/are not allowed to penetrate. These are tasks that everyone should engage in.

37

The previous chapter explored the plantation mistress trope in literature with an emphasis on narratives told from the perspective of white women. While *Property* featured a subversive white female slave owner, *The Wedding Gift* was a replication of the stereotype of white plantation mistresses as passive, weak, and uninformed. These representations of white women slave-owners differ from previous conceptions because of the reliance on postmodern creative interventions to depict women as slaves and owners simultaneously. This destabilized position demonstrates that literary white women slave-owners respond to their slave-owning duties from the perspective of both a slave and owner. Both texts also demonstrate the importance of women telling their own narratives, specifically in an American context where slavery is a taboo topic that many people shy away from.

This chapter focuses on representations of black women as slave-owners in literature and analyzes how race complicates this portrayal. The title of this chapter communicates black women's contradictory experiences as slaves and slave masters. Ownership is construed in the texts at hand as a survival tactic that black women must wield if they want to live through slavery's traumas. Black women slave-owners must survive a white male dominated slave system that undermines their power and does not provide them with the same respect that white male slave-owners are given. In *Wild Seed*, Anyanwu, an African immigrant, shapeshifts as a white male plantation owner to buy and free slaves. She uses her instincts and intellect that she developed as a slave to disrupt the plantation system. *Wild Seed* was published in 1980 when the post-civil rights era started to develop and writers began to play around with the slave narrative form. Unlike the rest of the texts in this project, it was not written in the new millennium, but it foreshadows a shift between representations of slavery during the civil rights era and after the post-civil rights era.

The Known World and *Cane River* exemplify a shift from portraying black people as triumphant slaves to imagining ways that they seized power and agency. Trudier Harris chronicles this shift as a movement from realism to more experimental forms of writing in the African American literary tradition, emphasizing how "the late twentieth century and early twenty-first-century writing could re-create and/or embellish [slavery] however they wished. This made possible revelations of unrecorded history and the mythology surrounding it, of instances in which enslaved persons bested their masters . . ." (176). Thus, the slave-owner becomes a literary figure that can be construed as anyone, including a black man or woman. This shift, I argue, occurred because the black literary imagination takes a turn toward postmodern conventions where characters are contradictions who are both oppressed and oppressors. At first glance, both novels seem to fit into the historical fiction genre but Tademy and Jones seem less concerned about being historically accurate and more concerned about exploring how the concept of black woman slave-owners complicates the slave-owner archetype and makes for a compelling story.

Edward P. Jones and Lalita Tademy utilize postmodern creative interventions, such as intertextuality and identity fluidity, in their portrayals of black women; and like *12 Years a Slave*, the current political climate seems to have influenced these portrayals. While Caldonia and Doralise participate in the exploitation of slaves, both characters are portrayed with sympathy despite their status as slave-owners. Although the black women slave-owners in these texts do not enjoy the same amount of power as their white counterparts, they are still participating in a system that dehumanizes black people regardless of their characterization as benevolent owners. This represents a shift from portrayals of black women as victims to colonizers. What are the limitations and politics behind portraying black women as colonizers? How does the twenty-first-century American cultural climate influence how black women slave-owners are characterized? This relates to Soyica Diggs Colbert's discussion of "neoliberal exceptionalism" where "the accumulation of a certain amount of property in a certain amount of time—by age forty—purchases a new configuration of blackness" in the twenty-first century (8). She references an interview with producer and artist Pharrell Williams who describes "the new black" as people like Oprah Winfrey, Lebron James, and Barack Obama who have achieved a plethora of success and fame (8). There are interesting ways in which Doralise Derbanne, a black woman slave-owner in *Cane River*, is classified as exceptional by her goddaughter, Suzette, who is enchanted by Doralise's ability to own slaves, property, and land. Within a slavery framework, Doralise represents neoliberal exceptionalism as a woman who Suzette sees as someone who has transcended her blackness. With a twenty-first-century focus on neoliberal exceptionalism, the slave-owner, a cultural trope which, until recently, did not feature many black women, becomes a character available to black women. In other words, the current cultural climate of the United States, one that focuses on the concept of colorblindness and neoliberal exceptionalism, allows for black women to be characterized as slave-owners more than they used to.

Cane River and *The Known World* function not only as responses to this cultural climate, but as responses to both *Roots* and *Gone with the Wind*, two prominent cultural artifacts about slavery. In *Cane River*'s introduction, Tademy questions *Gone with the Wind*'s portrayal of plantations, informing the reader how she "discovered that most plantations were not like the sprawling expanses of Tara in *Gone with the Wind* but were small, self-contained communities, surrounded by farms that were smaller still" (xii). Tademy represents a diverse range of slave-owners and slaves—some slave-owners are so poor that they can only afford one slave and a tiny amount of land. She takes a pluralistic, intertextual approach to slavery, emphasizing that *Gone with the Wind* portrays *one* possible representation of slavery rather than *the* representation. As discussed in the previous chapter, championing one narrative as the narrative is a problem, as it diminishes competing subjectivities. Tademy's argument is also an implicit indictment of *Gone with the Wind*'s large cultural capital—the novel and film permeate American popular cultural narratives of slavery, leaving very little room for other slavery representations. This massive following and recognition explains why African American authors, including Alice Walker and Malcolm X, are preoccupied with challenging and dismantling the stereotypes featured in Gone with the Wind. Tademy chastises *Gone with the Wind* later in the introduction when she discusses her women ancestors, observing how "They were not Mammy or Jezebel or Topsy, the slave images made safe and familiar in *Gone with the Wind* tradition. They were flesh-and-blood women who made hard choices, even in oppression" (xv). This quotation demonstrates Tademy's commitment to portraying black women as multidimensional and in direct opposition to texts like *Gone with the Wind* that stifle black women's subjectivity. Her emphasis on the "hard choices" her ancestors made is a stark contrast to the narratives about slavery that focus on black women's lack of agency and choices. Although her ancestors made hard choices, it appears as if they enjoyed a certain amount of privilege than other black women. Though this is a response to *Gone with the Wind*, it also encourages the reader to reconsider the African American literary tradition to provides safe or stilted characterizations of black women, focusing on the need to provide multiple, counternarratives of black subjectivity. The introduction also touches upon Tademy's "*Roots* trip to Louisiana" and the first time she went "back by choice" (xiii). Alex Haley's text has become synonymous with African American genealogy, and Tademy seeks to illuminate black women, who were not strong presences in *Roots*.[2] *Cane River* has been a part of *Oprah's Book Club* since 2001, and Oprah's website praises the book as "a compelling, heartfelt, and sweeping American saga" as well as "An epic work of fiction deeply rooted in historical fact [that] spans a hundred turbulent years to trace the lives of women who battled unspeakable injustices to create a legacy of hope and achievement." This blurb positions *Cane River* as the female counterpart of *Roots* with its emphasis on the text as an "America saga" as well as highlighting its temporal progression from the 1830s to the 1930s.

While the first chapter of this project explored texts that have not received an abundance of critical acclaim, *The Known World* has received several awards, including the 2004 Pulitzer Prize in Fiction, and is famous for its unorthodox approach to representing slavery in literature. Aptly described by Susan Donaldson (along with Martin's *Property*) as "postmodern novels written for a postmodern South and a postmodern age—with all the connotations of a loss of mastery that term 'postmodern' carries," *The Known World* provides a postmodern creative intervention onto the topic of slavery in fiction by depicting Manchester County, Virginia, as an area that reconciles contradictions about gender, race, class, and other identity categories. Scholars have debated how to classify *The Known World*, and it has been called a postmodern slave narrative, neo-slave-narrative, and historical novel. The text is a combination of these three entities, which makes it a perfect candidate for inclusion into the post-neo-slave narrative genre.

Both texts demonstrate that the most profound difference between white plantation mistresses and black plantation mistresses is that black women use their knowledge as former slaves or their close proximity to slaves, to penetrate the plantation hierarchy. Slaves utilize subversive communication styles to plan rebellions and disrupt the power slave-owners wield. It is this knowledge that helps black women become skilled slave-owners. In *Cane River*, Doralise convinces Eugent Daurat, who is a French white plantation owner, Philomene's father through the rape of her mother, Suzette, and Doralise's lover, to buy his son, Gerant, after their owner dies. She uses her relationship with both the slaves and the white elite to make this deal come into fruition. Not only does she get a new house slave for her plantation, but the deal also allows the slaves to think that she has their best interest, as they assume that Gerant is better off with her (157). In *The Known World*, Caldonia is born free, but she keeps Moses, one of her slaves, to continue keeping the slaves in line based on the false hope that she will marry him someday and make her the owner of the plantation. Moses thinks that this is a realistic proposition because Caldonia is a black woman, but he fails to realize, as Trudier Harris suggests "the impact of class and status on his aspirations. Caldonia may have sex with him "on the floor" but never invites him in her bed (190). Moses forgets that Caldonia is a slavemaster who from a higher class and she ends up marrying Louis, a slaveholder who is on the same elite status as her. Caldonia manipulates Moses into complying with her demands, and he would not have gotten ideas of transcending the plantation hierarchy if Caldonia were white and would have instead known that a marriage between owner and slave was impossible.

WHY *THE KNOWN WORLD* AND *CANE RIVER* ARE POST-NEO-SLAVE NARRATIVES

The primary argument of this chapter focuses on the need to classify *The Known World* and *Cane River* as post-neo-slave narratives, as several critics, such as Richard Schur, consider both texts as predominantly replications of history rather than the product of a twenty-first-century American culture that is preoccupied with colorblindness and a mistrust of the topic of slavery. Both texts use literary postmodern conventions blended with characteristics of the neo-slave narrative in order to challenge dominate cultural and historical narratives about slavery. I argue that they create alternative narratives that characterize black women as slave-owners who are content with the slave hierarchy and seek to hire their position in it instead of dismantling it. This differs from how some critics read these texts as I am placing these texts in conversation with popular cultural artifacts about slavery such as *Gone with the Wind* and *Roots*. My argument focuses on how *The Known World* and *Cane River* are not interested in creating *the* black woman slave-owner experience and care more about showing the diversity within slave-owning culture, which connects to postmodernism's emphasis on the plural rather than the singular.

This chapter also argues that when considering intersectionality, another postmodern approach to identity, both texts attempt to disrupt the traditional plantation mistress trope by demonstrating how it is a means of survival for black women. Slave-owning is a tactic that black women use to assert their freedom—by owning another human being, black women show that they have obtained a crucial facet of citizenship. While, arguably, white women did not need to become slave-owners to demonstrate their freedom, black women did, which challenges the conceptions of freedom featured in both neo-slave narratives and slave narratives. As the *Wild Seed* quotation in the title demonstrates, sometimes, for black women, it is owned or be owned, even if that is a problematic and reductive construction of freedom.

Neo-Slave Narratives

Among scholars, there are competing definitions of what constitutes a neo-slave narrative. Although there are competing definitions, most scholars agree that neo-slave narratives were produced during the civil rights era. Bell lays out his criteria for neo-slave narratives when discussing *Jubilee*: "Margaret Walker gives us our first major neoslave narrative: residually oral, modern narratives of escape from bondage to freedom" (289). Rushdy's definition is more specific and focuses on the first-person persona captured in neo-slave narratives. This first-person voice speaks to the witnessing and testifying that occurred in first person antebellum slave narratives; as in, the narrator was given more credibility if s/he could tell his or her own story. For the purpose of my project, I will use Bell's definition of neo-slave narratives for several reasons. First, authorship is mediated—similar to how slaves received outside help when crafting their narratives, the American writers, artists, musicians, and filmmakers that I examine use a team of people to help shape their texts. Second, not all of the texts I analyze are told in first person narration, but they do all feature someone who journeyed from bondage to freedom (and back to bondage, in some cases). Rushdy's analysis is still useful, and although this project speaks more to Bell's definition, I will include Rushdy in my dissertation.

Contemporary American texts such as *Cane River* and *The Known World* challenge conventions of the neo-slave narrative by dismantling the mimetic structure associated with the original genre. Rushdy defines the neo-slave narrative as "contemporary novels that assume the form, adopt the conventions, and take on the first person voice of the antebellum slave narrative" (3). Rushdy's analysis focuses on how the 1960s civil rights era shaped and informed the conventions of the neo-slave narrative. During this period, the antebellum slave narrative took on a new meaning, and the study of American slavery "was invigorated by a renewed respect for the truth and value of slave testimony, the significance of slave cultures, and the importance of slave resistance" (Rushdy 4). Activists, historians, and other cultural critics used the antebellum slave narrative as an example of history told from the perspective of the oppressed as well as an example of how they can fight for legislation that honored civil rights. In the twenty-first century, I argue that artists seem less concerned about accuracy and truth and are more interested in engaging with elements of fantasy.

The Postmodern Slave Narrative

A Timothy Spaulding's definition of the postmodern slave narrative focuses on the use of fantastic elements to disrupt the strict realism portrayed in slave narratives. Rather than mimic the form of slave narratives, which is what neo-slave-narratives do, postmodern slave narratives create "alternative and fictional historiography based on a subjective, fantastic, and anti-realistic representation of slavery" (2). Using this definition, Spaulding uses Toni Morrison's *Beloved* and Ishmael Reed's *Flight to Canada* as texts that exemplify elements of the postmodern slave narrative based on their ability to deploy "elements of the fantastic or metafiction in their texts" by forcing "us to question the ideologies embedded within the 'realistic' representation of slavery on traditional history and historical fiction" (2). The postmodern slave narrative is an attempt to write about the unknowable by using fantasy and questioning dominant historical narratives.

Tim Ryan, however, challenges the idea that the postmodern slave narrative can exist, claiming that critics "wish—understandably—to distinguish the qualities of postmodern fiction and the achievements of recent black novelists that critics have tended to understate drastically the degree to which there have always been dissenting historical counternarratives" (6). He contends that contemporary African American fiction about slavery is not inherently postmodern and challenges critics' attempts to "clarify what constitutes a postmodernist approach to the past [by overstating] what is distinctive and innovative about how writers engage with history in their work" (9). Because historical accounts of slavery are not monolithic or orthodox, he argues that a dominant narrative does not exist; rather, some narratives receive more cultural attention than others. This is in opposition to Spaulding's conception of the postmodern slave narrative, as Spaulding argues that postmodern slave narrative is an alternative to the dominant cultural narrative of slavery.

The definition of the postmodern slave narrative that is the most succinct, as well as relevant to this project, is Maria Seger's, who defines it as a "contemporary African American novel that engages formal elements of postmodernism and the original slave narrative in order to present an alternative historiography of slavery. Postmodern slave narratives, under my definition, regard both realism and objectivity with suspicion, cultivating authority over history through a variety of aesthetic and fictional means" (1192). This definition allows the inclusion of novels, such as *The Known World*, that do not, on the surface, explicitly engage in science fiction or fantasy into the genre.

While my definition of the post-neo-slave narrative appears similar to Seger's conception of the postmodern slave narrative, it differs in that I am more interested in how postmodern conventions alter the neo-slave-narrative as well as how the post-neo-slave narrative places literary texts in conversation with non-literary texts. In my project, it is through the portrayal of women that allows me to classify these texts as post-neo-slave narratives.

Representations of Black Women in Slavery

Most American literary representations of black women during slavery focus on their status as slaves. Phillis Wheatley, born in Africa and sold into slavery as a child, was an esteemed writer of poetry and letters. In her work, she portrays black slaves as noble, a direct contrast to the literary representations of slaves during this period. Harriet Wilson's *Our Nig: Sketches from the Life of a Free Black* (1859) is a semi-autobiographical account that details Frado's life as a servant for the Bellmont family. Frado is portrayed as a kind hard-worker who does not deserve the mistreatment she receives from Mrs. Bellmont. Wheatley and Wilson's work focuses on black women as victims of the slave system who are mistreated by white people.

In the nineteenth/early twentieth century, the trope of the mulatta woman in the cottage emerged, and multiracial women characters were known for their conflicting attitudes toward race and slavery. Paula Barnes describes this literary figure as "a slave woman placed in a cottage in an isolated setting at the behest of a white male who is most often her owner," emphasizing how

"The setting is an important element of the trope, for it provides protection and privacy for the mistress (and oftentimes her lover)." Barnes argues that William Wells Brown's *Clotel: or, The President's Daughter* typifies this trope through Clotel, one of the main characters whose attempts to escape society's rules about race and interracial relationships are unsuccessful when her white lover marries a white woman in order to further his political aspirations. This trope is also present through Harriet Jacobs's character in *Incidents in the Life of a Slave Girl* (1861), which chronicles Jacobs's life as a slave in the South to a freewoman in the North. In order to escape, she hides in plain sight by squatting in a tiny attic near her white male slavemasters' living quarters for seven years while writing letters from a fake New York address. She is tricked into living in a cottage by Dr. Flint, her white male slavemaster, when he threatens to separate her from her children. Unlike in Clotel, the cottage becomes a space where scheming and plotting occurs, as Jacobs starts planning her escape there. Hannah Crafts's *The Bondswoman Narrative* features Evelyn, a slave woman who is banished to live in a cottage by Mrs. Cosgrove, the plantation mistress of the mansion where Evelyn was squatting. This trope is challenged in *Cane River*, when Doralise Derbanne, a biracial woman, is given her own large home by her slaveholding white father, and successfully navigates slave and free society in Creole Louisiana.

Slave women continued to be the focus of many texts in the twentieth century, including *Roots* (1977) (and *Queen: The Story of an American Family* [1993], its spinoff about Alex Haley's grandmother), *Dessa Rose* (1990), *Jubilee* (1966), and *Beloved* (1987). Margaret Walker's *Jubilee* is credited as one of the first American novels to focus on black women's experiences during slavery. The novel is about Vyry Brown, a slave on her father's plantation, who lives through slavery and Reconstruction. Kizzy, the most prominent female character in *Roots*, is intelligent and hard-working, and she is sold to another plantation, away from her family, after she forges a travelling pass for one of her friends. She is raped by her new slavemaster and gives birth to Chicken George, who resembles his father in looks and actions. Although *Roots* focuses on men's experiences in slavery, Kizzy's story showed a renewed cultural interest in the plight of slave women. Sherley Anne Williams's *Dessa Rose* chronicles the titular character's journey from bondage to freedom. She is initially a fugitive slave who is captured and slated for execution before she escapes to a plantation owned by a white woman. *Beloved* is known for portraying Sethe as a complex black woman character who commits several tragic acts while attempting to flee from slavery. This is arguably one of the first times that a black woman slave is portrayed as both a victim and a perpetrator of violence against other black people. *Beloved* allowed for more nuanced portrayals of black slave women that questioned their actions and motives.

There is a preoccupation with the portrayal of black slave women as noble and always against the slavery system. There is rarely, however, a literary discussion of the ways in which they support the slave economy until recently. Anyanwu, the main character of Octavia Butler's *Wild Seed*, is a shapeshifter who occupies many competing subject positions throughout the novel. Anyanwu's position as a slave-owner and slave is fluid—at several points in the novel, she occupies both spaces. We can read this as a sign that intersectionality complicates the type of power that black women can have. Interestingly, Anyanwu is a shapeshifter who takes on the identity of a white male slave-owner. She creates a colony where she buys slaves and then frees them; this, however, is not as noble of a gesture as it seems. As the novel progresses, she becomes less sympathetic toward the slaves that she buys, and she believes in the institution of slavery enough to buy people. Anyanwu's identity as a slave-owner is based on her notion that slave owning is a masculine practice, which is why she shapeshifts into a white man instead of using her black female identity to own slaves. *The Known World* and *Cane River*, the subjects of this chapter, continues *Wild Seed*'s legacy by complicating black women characters' relationship with slavery and ownership. While both texts still characterize black women as victims, they highlight the methods black women slave-owners utilize to oppress other black people and increase their position in the plantation hierarchy.

Cane River's Postmodern Aesthetic

I consider *Cane River* a post-neo-slave narrative due to its postmodern approach to gender, race, and identity as well as its commitment to rewriting previous narratives about black women. Like the formation of the neo-slave narrative during the civil rights era, *Cane River* draws on conventions of postmodernity to provide a stronger depiction of black women during slavery. It draws from the current American cultural climate to provide an alternative to the dominant slavery narrative. *Cane River*'s postmodern aesthetic is debated among scholars; Schur's analysis of literature during the hip hop era diminishes *Cane River* as a text that has "retreated from hip-hop culture and hip-hop aesthetics as primary influences. They suggest a movement from layered samples, rhythmic asymmetries, and irony. To some, this work might reflect a return to more romantic or tragic narrative modes, which possess more confidence in literary representation to produce positive imagery" (171). Layered sampling and irony are conventions of postmodernity that actually are featured in *Cane River*. After Suzette is raped by Eugene, she gives birth to a son and wishes to name him Philomone. Elisabeth, Suzette's mother, reminds her that Gerant is the boy's name when they are in mixed company, which is also the name that he is referred to throughout the text by the omniscient narrator, hinting toward who the target audience for this text is. After Elisabeth corrects her, Suzette shakily protests with, "But he's mine" (59). This line is a sample from Toni Morrison's *Beloved* where, throughout the text, Sethe claims ownership over Beloved, stating that "Beloved, she my daughter. She's mine." Like Sethe, since Suzette, as a slave, does not have ownership over anything, the ability to call her son "mine" and name him how she wants exemplifies an attempt to exert agency. Sethe's decision to kill Beloved was a desperate move that intended to prevent her from experiencing slavery and also represents an act of agency. By using an intertextual approach to draw a parallel between Sethe's relationship with Beloved and Suzette's relationship with Gerant, *Cane River* demonstrates "that black women in the United States have been historically manipulated and made vulnerable through reproduction," as Gershun Avilez observes in her analysis of Aishah Rahman's *Unfinished Women* (110). She places *Cane River* in conversation with another text about slavery that engages with and dissects black women's experiences.

Cane River utilizes irony to draw attention to the denigration of black women's bodies through Louis Derbanne's conversation with Eugene. Louis, Doralise's father and Suzette's owner, acclimates Eugene to Louisiana Creole slave culture by discussing how "the plantation is the fulfillment of God's design" and explaining why slavery is necessary (31). As Suzette lights his cigarettes and pours his wine while being forcefully gazed upon by Eugene, Louis describes slavery as "the only workable system for cotton production, as good for our Negroes as it is for the whites. We took them out of Africa and lifted them up. The planters set the tone for the rest. Our burden is heavy" (55). The narrator then describes how Louis "shook his head sadly" (55). The irony is that Louis does not have any burdens to lift since he lives a leisure life that consists of wine and dinner parties. The heaviest burden he lifts is the wine bottle, and his heavy drinking causes an early death. Although Louis sincerely believes this, the reader is on Suzette's side and knows that what he says is not true, and Tademy uses irony as a literary technique to align the reader with Suzette; we are supposed to laugh at the irony of a member of the elite class complaining about carrying heavy burdens. Linda Hutcheon argues that postmodern irony is a "rhetorical and structural strategy of resistance and opposition," which confirms Tademy's usage of irony here as a method for deconstructing the white male plantation owner figure (12).

To further dissect Schur's argument about *Cane River*'s lack of twenty-first-century aesthetics, I argue that *Cane River* is not a narrative based on romantic narratives, as it is extremely clear about the brutal methods used to violate women, and the imagery in the texts is not as positively as his analysis suggests. While talking with Philomene about her husband, Clement, who was sold to a plantation in Virginia, Suzette tells Philomene that "At least you know what it is to want a man, and have him want you back. That's something I never tasted, the choosing of it, the pleasure of it" (218). Suzette suggests that Philomene was lucky to have a husband, even if it was for a short period, because she never had the opportunity to choose a partner. This passage provides a tragic outlook on love and romance as well as demonstrates Suzette's bitterness toward her daughter. The text seems devoid of the romantic narrative mode that Schur observes.

Nghana Lewis argues against Schur as well, commenting that "These observations are quite peculiar, given that these novels propel black women on journeys toward self-actualization through events that implicate stock elements of hip hop storytelling. Each novel focuses upon questions of black female subjectivity that intersect with the central—and critiques—of mainstream hip hop's commodification of black women's bodies." *Cane River* is preoccupied with the treatment of black women's bodies as property and an object subject to commodification. Philomene decides to seduce Narcisse Fredieu, a white widowed plantation owner who is superstitions and believes the premonitions that Philomene feeds to him. Although Narcisse will not free her and her children, she convinces him to build a cottage on his property, teach his children how to read and write, and let his children take his last name. After the birth of Emily, Philomene reflects on her decision to become a mother, observing how "Despite the unrelenting demands of the newborn, she had grown increasingly optimistic about the future, and the recovery from this childbirth had been swift. Her body seemed to be well engineered for the business of producing babies" (247). Philomene's body is described in impersonal, mechanical language, as if she is a robot and not an actual human being. "Well engineered" suggests that she was constructed specifically for giving birth, which is how black women were treated during slavery and connects to how she was produced by the rape of her mother. Although this passage treats Philomene's body as a product, Philomene describes herself as being "optimistic about the future," which suggests that this is a form of agency and power. She turns the act of giving birth as a gesture that can benefit her. However, Philomene, later in the text, acknowledges that agency for black women can only look like this within the slave system, as this is the type of resistance that also benefits the white male slave-owner. This passage exemplifies debates about hip hop culture and its ability to empower black women. The last chapter of this project highlights these conversations and suggests that black women can draw upon slavery conventions to subvert the sexism rampant in hip hop. Black women rappers have found strategies to critique the commodification of black women's bodies, similar to what Tademy does in *Cane River*.

Similarly to Lewis, I challenge Schur's argument about *Cane River* by suggesting that *Cane River* is the epitome of a novel about slavery written with postmodern aesthetics and the layered sampling that Schur values in Morrison's work. *Cane River* samples, and subsequently flips, the plantation mistress, mammy, and tragic mulatta tropes that are important facets of twentieth century literary representations of slavery. Tademy uses twenty-first-century postmodern conventions to rewrite these tropes and provide a complex picture of black women's subjectivity, which is also a goal put forth by many black women rappers. Suzette, who is often described as cocoa colored, chastises the white elites that she works for while simultaneously becoming disappointed that her daughter is marrying a field slave. The mulatta in a cottage is an American literary cultural trope outlined earlier in this chapter, and Tademy challenges this trope through Philomene's insistence that Narcisse build a cottage for her family that is on his property rather than away from the Creole society. She rewrites black women as flawed and complicated while placing her text is direct opposition to *Gone with the Wind*.

Tademy's concern with the imagery used to portray black women forms the basis of purpose for writing *Cane River*. While Schur argues that *Cane River* "deemphasize[s] fragmentation and the power of popular culture in shaping African American identity and culture" and is "less explicitly invested in claiming ownership over the American cultural imagination or redistributing property rights. Rather, they offer smaller narratives that chart the complexity of African American life and seek to represent the trauma of history," I read *Cane River* as attempting to overwrite popular cultural narratives of African American identity in addition to demonstrating black women's traumatic history, rather than choosing to focus on one over the other. Throughout the text, Tademy is explicit in highlighting how the *gens de couleur libre* (free people of color) participate in the oppression and exploitation of slaves. When Elisabeth and Suzette attend the *gens de couleur libre* church, Elisabeth grunts about how "the free people of color who built that church own more slaves than the Derbannes. They go by their own rules" (7). The free people of color are referred to using French, not English, which is a linguistic example of how this population is separated from other black people within the Creole community. By doing this, Tademy portrays a multitude of black identities and examines the colorism and discrimination that is rampant among people of color. Tademy is representing the trauma of history in conjunction with claiming ownership over American cultural imagination or redistributing property rights.

Doralise Derbanne and Creole Slave-Owning

Although Doralise Derbanne is not related to Tademy, she details her interactions with her ancestors and includes historical documentation about her such as her divorce papers and proof of slave-owning practices. Doralise is the biracial daughter of Louis Derbanne, the white male slave-owner who owns Suzette, Elisabeth, and their family prior to his death. She is Suzette's godmother, and she calls her *marraine*, the French word for godmother. Like other free people of color, this French name denotes Doralise's distinction from other black people, representing her superior status. Doralise is despised by Francoise Derbanne, Louis's wife, because he freed her when she was a child and gave her property, slaves, and his last name. As Suzette references throughout the text, those with last names are part of the elite class, and she longs to have a last name of her own.

The reader is first introduced to Doralise through Suzette's explanation that Doralise occupies "a middle place, not as high as the white Derbannes or the Fredieus and not as low as any of those she sponsored as godmother from the house or the quarter" (10). Although Doralise was given Louis's last name, Suzette is careful to make a distinction between the white Derbannes and Doralise, demonstrating her understanding of the plantation hierarchy. The word choice she uses to describe Doralise's relationship to the slaves, "sponsored," sounds as if Doralise is treating the slaves as a charity case. This is similar language used by Westerners who donate money toward children in non-Western countries as well as mirrors the type of language slave-owners in the text use to describe their relationship to slaves. The capitalist, economic language further elevates Doralise as a slave-owner whose money allows her a certain amount of power and control, furthering her representation under the neoliberal exceptionalism rubric, which brings Doralise's character into a twenty-first-century context.

Suzette develops a crush on Nicolas, another *gens de coleur libre*, and characterizes him as different and more like her Doralise, emphasizing how he never looks "past her as if she were not really there," which demonstrates her desire to be visible and recognized by the free people of color (22). Suzette longs for a church wedding with Nicolas as her husband, and when Elisabeth discusses how this dream cannot become a reality, Suzette explains how "*Marraine* Doralise wasn't born free . . . but she's free now and was married in the church" (23). The church represents a space that legitimizes citizenship and freedom—to have a church wedding is to become a visible and legal member of the Creole community. Doralise's freedom is solidified by her ability to have a church wedding. Suzette is, once again, attuned to the plantation hierarchy and the material symbols of freedom. Elisabeth counters Suzette's response with "M'sieu had his own reasons to make her free and set her up to marry," heavily implying that Doralise gained her status because Francoise, Louis's wife, cannot have children and carry on his legacy. As Hazel Carby argues, white women of the elite planter class "were viewed as the means of the consolidation of property through the marriage of alliance between plantation families, and they gave birth to the inheritors of that property," which demonstrates how white women were tasked with creating citizens of the elite (24). Francoise, thus, is seen as a failed plantation mistress due to her inability to reproduce and continue the Derbanne bloodline; Doralise, then, jumps ahead of her on the plantation hierarchy due to her reproduction capabilities, complicating Carby's assessment that "black women gave birth to property and, directly, to capital itself in the form of slaves" (25). In Cane River's literary world, as well as in twenty-first-century representations of slave women, black women can become skilled slave-owners who can increase their positioning during slavery, illuminating a key difference between neo-slave narratives and post-neo-slave narratives.

Suzette idealizes Doralise Derbanne as a free woman of color who uses her sexuality to her advantage and describes her as "a dignified, well-bred woman, everything Suzette wished she could be" (71) as well as "a free colored woman, one of the Ones with Last Names" who had "land, money, and slaves of her own" (72). When Doralise arrives at church with a black eye after her first husband beat her, Suzette compares her to "a ripe peach she had once found on the ground in the big garden, seemingly so perfect until she'd picked it up and exposed an oozing, rotten wound on the underside" (72). This description foreshadows Doralise's representation throughout the rest of the text; the comparison of Doralise to a rotten fruit is indicative of the attitude residents take toward her when she lives with Eugene after her divorce. She is also similar to the Adam and Eve biblical story, which is reference frequently in texts about slavery. Suzette represents Adam and is deeply enchanted by her godmother even after the warning signs that Doralise may not be as trustworthy as she idealizes her as. This description of Doralise also encourages the reader to question Doralise's motives as well as remind us that as a slave-owner, she participates in slavery's capitalist enterprises; Doralise's slave-ownership represents her "rotten wound" and makes her character less admirable.

Although Suzette has created a perfect image of Doralise in her mind, one that may not represent how she really is, I argue that the texts shows that Doralise barely knows much about her, which breaks the perception of Suzette and Doralise as close. When Suzette becomes pregnant with Philomene after being raped by Eugene, Doralise tells her to "be more careful" while asking if Suzette is fifteen or sixteen—Suzette is actually seventeen (72). The inability to know Suzette's age demonstrates that these two are not close as Suzette claims they are while showing how Doralise is no different than the other *gens de coleur libre* who ignore her. Her advice to tell Suzette to "be more careful" assumes that Suzette has a choice and can refuse Eugene's advances. This exchange represents the distance between Doralise and Suzette, as well as slave-owner and slave, while complicating Doralise's character. Like many representations of plantation mistresses, Doralise is a victim of abuse who must exploit slaves in order to maintain her position in the plantation hierarchy. Despite Doralise's polite insults, Suzette asks her to be her baby's godmother, which she accepts, which illuminates Suzette's desperation for the *gens de coleur libre*'s approval.

Although the previous sections appear to set Doralise up as a Jezebel, Tademy is careful to not characterize her as sexually promiscuous and highlights how sexuality is used as a tool for gaining power within the plantation hierarchy. After Doralise is granted a divorce from her husband, which is unheard of during this period, she lives with Eugene, who calls her "a free woman of color who filled his days and frequented his dreams at night," and the Creole community shuns people who live together without being married, especially interracial unmarried couples (127–8). Eugene idolizes her, like Suzette, and sees Doralise as an image rather than an actual person. After Doralise questions his loyalty to her, Eugene "went down to the courthouse again to gift her his land and his house, to convince her just how sincere she was" (128). This exemplifies Doralise's usage of sexuality to gain even more property and power. She flips the script on Eugene by putting him in the subservient role, as he is the one who is tasked with convincing her of his sincerity. This also represents Tademy's attempts to restructure the plantation hierarchy by visualizing ways that black women may have used the small amount of agency they had to increase their position. Eugene must prove his sincerity through property rather than other material symbols of love, complicating common ideas of romance and love. Doralise's actions set a precedent for other black women, as Philomene decides that she wants to manipulate Narcisse into building her a cottage and teaching their children how to read/write the same "way her *marraine*, Doralise, had done it" (149).

The roles between Doralise and Eugene are flipped—Eugene becomes the slave while Doralise continues to increase her financial power as a slaveowner, which are Tademy's provocative attempts to complicate racial and gender roles during slavery. When Eugene and Doralise end their relationship, Eugene moves back to France without any American property in his name, as he signed it over to Doralise, and the small amount of power that he did have in the Creole community no longer exists. Their relationship distanced Eugene from the white elite, as he was no longer the mysterious French bachelor he was when he first arrived, and Doralise succeeded in dismantling any connections he had. I read this situation as Doralise's attempts to repay Eugene back for raping Suzette, as he left the United States as desolate and disgraced, and Suzette appreciates that she did "more for [Philomene] and Gerant than M'sieu Eugene ever did" (156). This further complicates Doralise's characterization and thrusts her into the anti-hero role, a role that, recently, has been typified by white men.

The Deconstruction of the Tragic Mulatta in a Cottage Trope

Cane River is in conversation with eighteenth and nineteenth century African American texts that featured the mulatta in the cottage trope where the cottage symbolized a form of excommunication from the larger slave society for the purposes of protection or exploitation, sometimes a combination of both. *Cane River* illuminates this trope through Philomene and Doralise. Philomene, inspired by her godmother, uses her reproduction abilities as a method for convincing Narcisse to provide her family with a better life. Philomene's ability to negotiate with Narcisse represents her mastery of the slave system, as she sets herself up as a prize that he must win (234). The cottage becomes a political space that symbolizes Philomene's negotiation skills as well as a revision of the tragic mulatta trope. Since this scene occurs in 1861, in the midst of the Civil War, Philomene uses the current political situation as another method for bribing Narcisse, as the Creole community is not confident that their way of life will survive after the war. She offers Narcisse a legacy through reproduction as a way to better her position. When Philomene gives birth to Narcisse's daughter, Philomene boldly tells him that "her name is Emily Fredieu. . . . She must never work in the field" (244). Emily becomes "one of those with a last name," the elite class who are revered by Suzette and Philomene throughout the text. Philomene draws a distinction between the field and the house slave, knowing that those who work in the house have a higher chance of planning successful rebellions due to their proximity to the slave-owners. These are common negotiation tactics for black women characters, as several black women in this project have similar aspirations as Philomene.

Traditionally, the cottage is a space that represents isolation and despair, but *Cane River* complicates this idea by demonstrating how the cottage is a visible space that represents power. Unlike the cottage in *Clotel*, Philomene's cottage is on the Fredieu plantation and is a part of the Creole community. This exemplifies another trope that *Cane River* flips, and Tademy uses postmodern literary techniques to turn the tragic mulatta in a cottage trope into a symbol of empowerment and subversion. Similarly, Jones flips several American cultural tropes and narratives in *The Known World*, and the goal of both novels is to disassociate these tropes and narratives from the usual connotations associated with them.

The Known World and Black Women Slave-Owners

Like *Cane River*, *The Known World* portrays slave culture through competing narratives that challenge the dominant American narrative of slavery, and Jones blurs the boundaries between black and white, slave and free, and wealthy and poor. Their postmodern approaches to the topic of slavery provides us with an alternative lens for viewing representations of slavery and the plantation hierarchy. *The Known World* features two prominent black women slave-owners, Caldonia and Maude, who are more interested in keeping the slave system intact rather than dismantling it, which challenges representations of black women in popular novels like *Gone with the Wind*. In addition to being slave-owners, black women hold various positions of power in Jones's conception of Manchester County, Virginia; Fern Elston, in addition to being a slave-owner, educates free black people, which allows her the ability to teach whatever narratives she sees fit. She teaches black people to become sharper and smarter slave-owners, with Robbins, Henry's slaveowner before he was freed, specifically choosing her as Henry's teacher due to her ability to teach him "how to conduct himself in Virginia" (127), and free black people become better businesspeople. As Harris observes, Henry's education "adds separation between him and his parents" and increases the distance between slave and free, which Fern contributed to (184). I argue that this conception of education complicates prior slave narratives where slaves were not allowed to learn how to read and write for fear that they would rebel; instead, *The Known World* treats education as a strategy black people can use to force themselves into the planter class.

Fern works within a white plantation slave system while claiming to dislike white people, demonstrating her hypocritical and precarious position in the hierarchy. Although Fern is extremely light, she insists that "it had never crossed [her] mind to pass as white. Not caring very much for white people, she saw no reason to become one of them" (130). While Fern is an active member of the free black community in Manchester County, she distinguishes herself from white people, insisting that black slave-owners are a separate class; yet, she shows disdain for darker skinned black people. This passage exemplifies the type of irony that makes *The Known World* a post-neo-slave narrative—it is ironic that Fern does not want to become white when, through her actions, she tries to keep the white plantation system intact. When Fern decides to free Jebediah, her dark-skinned slave, she misspells "manumit" in the freedom papers, and David Ikard assesses Fern's mistake as "a tragicomic joke . . . Despite being a lauded teacher and moralist, she does not know the proper spelling or grammatical usage of a word that means 'to set free from slavery'" (82). As the educator of free black people and future slave-owners, Fern's misspelling represents her misunderstanding of slavery as well as places her in the position of the illiterate slave, as slaves were expected to have misspellings when they forged their freedom papers. She occupies a contradictory space between slave and slave-owner with her characterization as a slave negatively influencing her mastery of slave-ownership.

Although Fern is often likened to a slave, her inability to empathize with slaves forces the reader to see the irony of her situation. As Fern is having a conversation with other free black people about slavery, she insists that "if I were in bondage I would slash my master's throat on the first day. I wonder why they all have not risen up and done that" (288). Not only does this perspective ignore the slave rebellions that were discussed in the text, including a story of a white woman slave-owner whose two slaves forced her into slavery after her husband died, but it demonstrates Fern's inability to view slavery as a large economic system. Her comment has a judgmental, rather than sympathetic, tone regardless of Fern's inability to see how she is often placed on the same level as slaves. The exchange with Jebediah transformed Fern from the educated slave-owner to the illiterate slave, complicating her perceived mastery of slavery while making Jebediah the metaphorical slave-owner. Fern's supposed contradictory characterization is an example of postmodern identity where polar opposite identity categories exist within one person, as she occupies the slave/slave-owner, black/white, illiterate/educated, and rich/poor spaces simultaneously. A key characteristic of postmodern works, Linda Hutcheon argues is its ability "to fragment or at least to render unstable the traditional unified identity or subjectivity of character" (90). Fern's destabilized character epitomizes this conception of identity, as her multiple subject positions are constantly competing. Through characters like Fern, Jones takes a postmodern approach to identity, one that illuminates their imperfect, complex subject positions.

Inheriting Slave-Owning through a Black Matriarchal Lineage

Free black women in *The Known World* are multidimensional characters whose victimhood is complicated by their oppression of others, which is a narrative that challenges most representations of black women in slavery. Caldonia epitomizes this theory; she is born free and becomes the sole slave-owner on her plantation after Henry, her husband, dies. Her mother, Maude, is a slave-owner who killed her father because he wanted to free their slaves. Due to this legacy, Caldonia learned that slave-owning is crucial part of a plantation mistress' identity and she must master it. Although Shauna Morgan Kirlew argues that Caldonia and other "free black women of wealth also attempted to imitate their white counterparts," I argue that Caldonia is not following white women; rather, she is emulating her mother. In the slave system, children inherited their slave status from the mother, and Jones flips this paradigm by having Caldonia follow her matriarchal lineage and become a slave-owner. After Henry's death, Maude encourages Caldonia not to sell the land and slaves, reasoning that Caldonia's legacy, as well as hers, "meant slaves and land, the foundation of wealth" (180). As Kirlew argues, this moment represents Maude's realization that, for black people, there is a thin line between slave and free, and owning slaves a way to distinguish between those two subject positions. Caldonia eventually agrees with her mother, stating that "Henry worked too hard to give me all of this. I would not squander it away, not in any way you could imagine. I know my duty to what he left me. However much I am Papa's daughter, *I am just as much your daughter*" (183, my emphasis). This passage demonstrates that Caldonia's need to please her mother, rather than her emulation of white women, is what prevents her from selling her slaves. Although in true postmodern identity fashion, Caldonia is conflicted between her patriarchal lineage and matriarchal lineage, she ultimately sides with her mother and realizes that she cannot keep her elite status if she is no longer a slave-owner. While slave-ownership is a symbol of hegemonic structures, Jones shows that while some similarities except between white and black women slave-owners, the free black women of *The Known World* are distinguished from white women, which illuminates the text's goal of showing a multitude of experiences during slavery. Thus, black women slave-owners might have some characteristics that are informed by white womanhood but are ultimately different in many ways due to race intersecting with their slave-owner identity.

Although a life of leisure is supposed to be a symbol of the slave-owning class's power, Maude complicates this dynamic when she decides to poison her husband, Tilmon. After Tilmon tells Maude that he plans on freeing the slaves, she devises a plan to poison him: "But she had poisoned Tilmon before anything like that could happen. Arsenic pie. Arsenic coffee. Arsenic meat. The servants had thought she had gone mad wanting to do all the cooking for her husband" (184). Since cooking is normally a task done by slaves, Maude transforms into a slave to kill her husband, further complicating the boundaries between free black woman and slave. To continue her life of leisure, she had to take the domestic space away from the slaves by cooking his food, which caused the slaves to likened her rejection of comfort and leisure to madness. This passage also refers to slaves as "servants," which is Maude's attempt to disassociate her cooking duties from slavery, which is ironic when considering that the reason why she becomes a cook is because she wants to keep slavery alive. This also represents a reversal of a scenario that is common in slavery representations; usually, slaves have to find creative methods for escaping and rebelling, such as Harriet Jacobs writing letters "from" New York when she was squatting only a few feet away from her slavemaster and Angela Davis's study that details how slave women poisoned their masters, but Maude flips this scenario by poisoning her husband to ensure that slavery will continue to thrive. This exemplifies another instance of black women's subjectivity and Jones's ability to complicate common tropes about slavery.

After slaves begin escaping from Caldonia's plantation, slave patrollers begin to question Caldonia's slave mastery, which is reminiscent of how black women's skills are scrutinized more than their white and male counterparts, and this demonstrates the inequality among slave-owners. Travis, a white patroller, complains about Caldonia's lack of slave-owning skills and suggests that somebody "should close the gate at her place, or teach her how to own a slave. A man dies and a woman runs his place to the ground" since she is making their jobs harder (348). The patrollers are running out of resources and cannot catch slaves as efficiently as they used to. Harris reads Travis's assessment of Caldonia's skills "even more negatively given the fact that Caldonia is not a white woman," which "continues to locate 'rightful' ownership with males" (193). Travis's comments reinforce the idea that slave-ownership is a masculine practice that women, specifically black women, do not possess the necessary skills to succeed at. This is a peculiar moment in the text, as it asks the reader to recognize Travis's sexism and arguably defend a black woman who is engaging in the commodification of human beings. It forces the reader to grapple with the question of whether or not we *want* a black woman to master the art of slave owning and disprove Travis's assessments. This specific moment is when Caldonia loses the respect of everyone around her—although sexism and gender roles may contribute to why she is not as feared as her husband was, being a slave-owner who oppresses other black people complicates how readers should respond to her, which contributes to the novel's uncomfortable tone.

Transitioning from Literary Post-Neo-Slave Narratives to Visual Ones

Cane River and *The Known World* highlight the multitude of experiences during slavery by dismantling the idea that there is one representation of slavery rather than many. They focus on providing counternarratives that challenge the singular American narrative of slavery experience from both the slave and slave-owner perspective. Both texts accomplish these goals through an intertextual approach that places them in direct conversation with other texts about slavery. Oprah's Book Club markets *Cane River* as "the female *Roots*," which highlights *Roots*'s focus on masculinity while marketing the novel to people who are familiar to *Roots*. This is even more apparent through Tademy's many references to *Roots*, *Gone with the Wind*, *Beloved*, and other representations of slavery. *The Known World* and *Cane River* question common conceptions of freedom, education, and discrimination and asks readers to reconsider their stances on these issues in fascinating ways.

While the first two chapters of this project focus on literature, the next two chapters will analyze slavery images featured in film and music as well as explore the differences and relationships between visual and literary representations of slavery. A crucial element of post-neo-slave narratives is the emphasis on placing literary and non-literary texts in conversation with each other. Due to the interconnectedness of different genres in twenty-first-century culture, as demonstrated by the how often the literary texts in this project reference visual culture and vice versa, it is imperative that a new genre of slavery representations is created to account for this complexity. The post-neo-slave narrative fills this crucial space by demonstrating the intertextual nature of literature and visual culture in slavery representations.

NOTES

1. I am down for reclaiming the term "mesearch." It is catchier and more appealing than "autoethnography."

2. Although *Queen*, one of the sequels to *Roots*, focuses on Alex Haley's biracial grandmother, it is not as popular or well-known in the United States. The book and film did not come close to reaching the record-shattering numbers that *Roots* obtained. In *Roots*, although Kizzy, Kunta Kinte's daughter, has a few sections that focus on her, Kunta Kinte is the cultural figure that most people associate with the book and film.

Chapter 3

"You will sell the negress!"

Revising Representations of Women in Django Unchained and 12 Years a Slave

On "My Momma Told Me," a podcast hosted by Langston Kerman that explores black conspiracy theories, Kerman and guest Michelle Buteau explore the theory that black slaves scattered when they laughed to avoid causing commotion and drawing attention to themselves. During their discussion, Buteau brings up the idea that slavery is rarely portrayed with lightness, nor that slaves had tender, humorous moments where they could just "be." *Django Unchained* is one of the few examples of a mainstream film that depicts slavery through humor and cheesiness. Although Quentin Tarantino utilizes multiple film genres to portray slavery, the tone is campier than most depictions. Critics bashed Tarantino for his unserious treatment of slavery, with Spike Lee declaring that "American slavery was not a Sergio Leone Spaghetti Western. It was a holocaust. My ancestors are slaves. Stolen from Africa. I will honor them." I argue that *Django Unchained* is a post-neo-slave narrative for the reasons that Lee highlights—it attempts to disrupt the usual American film portrayals of slavery by meshing multiple genres and perspectives.

In the previous two chapters, I focus on literary texts within the post-neo-slave narrative genre, and the next two chapters will examine the visual culture aspect of post-neo-slave narratives. Including visual and audio texts, such as film and music, into the canon provides a more holistic picture of slavery depictions in the twenty-first century as well as places them in conversation with literary texts and challenges standard genre conventions. Neo-slave-narratives were a response to the renewal of interest in slavery depictions during the civil rights era, and I argue that post-neo-slave narratives are a response to the twenty-first-century's cultural climate—what does slavery mean to contemporary artists, writers, and filmmakers? How do conventions of postmodernism influence depictions of slavery? How have conceptions of racial and gender identity changed since the civil rights era, and how does this influence how slavery is represented in visual culture? How does the twenty-first-century focus on neoliberal exceptionalism, as outlined in chapter 2, change artists' representations of slavery?

This chapter continues to engage with Camilla Dacey-Groth's conception of the slaveholder narrative by examining how it is configured in film.[1] The purpose of slaveholder narratives is to involve white American artists in the monumental task of dealing with slavery and its legacies. How do twenty-first-century filmmakers utilize the slaveholder experience in their productions? This chapter will also focus on postmodern techniques filmmakers utilize to construct the plantation mistress as a slave-owner, which is an aspect of their identity that addresses the concerns Dacey-Groth has about the sanitization of American depictions of slavery. Dacey-Groth's conception of the slaveholder narrative focuses on white Americans, and I want to complicate her definition by arguing that both *Django Unchained* and *12 Years a Slave* demonstrate the crucial need to the tell the story of women in positions of power, especially black women, slaveholders. Although *12 Years a Slave* (2014) and *Django Unchained* (2012) are narratives told from the perspective of black male slaves (Solomon Northup and Django, respectively), both films portray white and black women as active, willing participants in the exploitation of slaves and are explicit in their implication of women in contributing to the slave system. In the context of these two films, the plantation mistress trope is further debunked—she is no longer weak, passive, and oblivious but is rather cunning, devious, and masterful. The debunking of this trope is possible due to the freedom allowed by the post-neo-slave narrative—since identity is fluid and characters frequently shift between multiple, competing subject positions, postmodern concepts of identity and power make it possible to construct women, specifically black women, as colonizers.

Including film illuminates the post-neo-slave narrative by providing visual representations of slavery, and it is crucial to interrogate visual imagery that reaches a mass audience. Many popular cinematic films and television series featuring slavery, such as *Gone with the Wind* (1939) and *Roots* (1977), were book adaptations. Several critics, including Miriam Thaggert and William Foster, have criticized *Gone with the Wind* for romanticizing southern antebellum culture and flippantly treating slavery as unserious. Twenty-first-century representations of slavery are challenging and dismantling this romanticization, as I highlighted in chapter 2. Any romance that occurs in *12 Years a Slave* is cloaked with depressing imagery, such as the dark colors used to visualize Solomon's sexual encounter with a woman slave at the beginning of the film. *Django Unchained* uses humor as a strategy for making fun of Southern material culture; however, at times, this makes some characters, particularly Calvin Candie, seem misguided and likeable rather than cruel and heartless.[2]

This chapter also demands a further exploration of the connection between the postmodern slave narrative and the neo-slave narrative. The postmodern slave narrative and neo-slave narrative are often discussed in opposition rather than in unison. Scholars treat the postmodern slave narrative and neo-slave narrative as separate genres with no connection to each other. The original conception of the neo-slave narrative is altered by postmodernity while simultaneously providing a critique of postmodernism. In addition, a neo-slave narrative focuses on a literary character's journey from bondage to freedom but postmodern conceptions of both identity and genre allow the new post-neo-slave narrative genre to include visual and audio cultural artifacts such as film and music. This chapter treats *Django Unchained* and *12 Years a Slave* as post-neo-slave narratives due to the postmodern creative interventions the writers and directors make when reimagining slavery. I argue that postmodernity shapes the methods filmmakers use to visualize slavery—both films use music, juxtaposition, and clothing to align twenty-first-century America with its slavery roots.

DJANGO UNCHAINED, 12 YEARS A SLAVE, AND POSTMODERN CREATIVE INTERVENTIONS

I chose these two films as the focus of this chapter due to their, on the surface, drastically different approaches to the representation of slavery on film. *Django Unchained* encompasses the fantastical elements of postmodern slave narratives that A. Timothy Spaulding defines, as it "rejects the boundaries of narrative realism" (1) and engages with "aspects of postmodern subjectivity, history, and textuality by examining the instability of our narrative representation of the past" (3). *12 Years a Slave*, however, is rooted in a "realistic" representation of slavery since its referent is Solomon Northup's famous slave narrative, but as Stephanie Li observes, director Steve McQueen, screenwriter John Ridley, and cinematographer Sean Bobbitt take creative liberties with the original text by including scenes not featured in the book as well as illuminating peripheral women characters such as Patsey, Mistress Shaw, and Mistress Epps.

The departure from the original text is where postmodern conceptions of identity come into play, as constructions of female identity are based on postmodern ideas of exceptionalism and mastery. When discussing conceptions of black identity in the new millennium, Soyica Diggs Colbert argues that some contemporary black artists, such as artist Pharrell Williams, are defining blackness based on "neoliberal exceptionalism," where black celebrities' ability to accumulate wealth is a sign that it is time to "forget the old black that equated blackness with slavery, loss, or domination . . . " (8). *12 Years a Slave*, however, marries black exceptionalism with slavery and mastery through the characterization of Mistress Shaw. Rather than treating black identity as either/or, *12 Years a Slave* uses postmodern techniques to demonstrate that these identity categories are both/and. Mistress Shaw transforms into a slave-owner by mastering the slave system, demonstrating her exceptional ability to acquire wealth and freedom. The filmmakers' decision to illuminate Mistress Shaw is an example of twenty-first-century notions of identity that are based on fluidity and destabilization.

What interests me about these films is how both engage with the fantastic and the real simultaneously—scholars often praise *Django Unchained* for its playful take on slavery while *12 Years a Slave* is heralded as a firm, realistic representation of slavery; however, I am interested in the moments where *Django Unchained* engages in realism and *12 Years a Slave* dabbles in fantasy, as this is what makes them perfect candidates for inclusion into the post-neo-slave narrative genre. I argue that they challenge standard conceptions of what representations of slavery should look like by playing around with genre conventions. In *12 Years a Slave*, the fantastical moments are included because of our twenty-first-century political climate—black women characters such as Patsey and Mistress Shaw are illuminated because black feminists demand more inclusion of black women's experiences into literature, film, and other genres. Though Spike Lee and other critics have chastised *Django Unchained* for its historical inaccuracies and perceived offensiveness, the moments in the film that "are true to slavery" relate to the treatment of black women—Broomhilda, in particular, is a reminder that black women were raped and abused during slavery, and although the film is not told from her perspective, she is constructed as a black woman *worth saving*, complicating the perception Kimberlé Crenshaw and other black feminists highlights that black women are incapable of being victims. Broomhilda's victimization, however, is complicated by her construction as different than other slave women due to her fluency in German and her characterization as a comfort slave. Comfort slaves were treated as prostitutes whose owners pimped them out to buyers, and the slave-owner received money for the transaction. Django implies that only attractive women are allowed to become comfort slaves.

In addition, each film features women plantation owners—Lara in *Django Unchained* and Mistress Epps and Mistress Shaw in *12 Years a Slave*—who simultaneously illuminate and resist the plantation mistress trope that is the focal point of this entire project. Although the past few years have seen an increase of scholarship about these films, most scholars do not focus on the white women characters—while some scholarship exists on Mistress Epps, there is even less about Lara, probably due to her lack of exposure in the film. Most scholarship discusses their reliance on their male counterparts instead of how they attempt to construct an identity separate and in conjunction with men. My literary analysis highlights the integral roles played by the characterizations of Mistress Shaw, Mistress Epps, and Lara and places them in the broader context of the plantation mistress trope as a crucial figure in American film and culture. Both films portray these characters as active participants in the financial exchange of slaves, and in representing this direct and explicit participation in the economic aspects of slavery, the films challenge and revise the romantic plantation mistress trope associated with Scarlett O'Hara and Julie Marsden. In addition to challenging the plantation mistress trope, *Django Unchained* classifies Broomhilda as a damsel in distress, a trope that rarely features black women characters, and I argue that when considering previous renditions of this trope, *Django Unchained* shows that black women are worth saving.

Why Every Depiction of Slavery Is Not a Neo-Slave Narrative

Marrying the postmodern slave narrative and the neo-slave narrative together to create the post-neo-slave narrative is necessary in order to understand representations of slavery in the twenty-first century. *Django Unchained* and *12 Years a Slave* have both been described as postmodern slave narratives and neo-slave narratives by Lesel Dawson and Stephanie Li separately. It is insufficient to describe these films as postmodern slave narratives and neo-slave narratives, as the original conception of these genres focuses on literary texts that are not created during the twenty-first century. Post-neo-slave narratives differ from other conceptions of slave narratives in that visual genres are included into the canon, providing a clearer understanding of twenty-first-century slavery representations and genre conventions. Including film into this genre provides the literary studies field with a broader picture of how slavery is represented in genres outside of literature. Providing a postmodern framework for viewing identity also allows us to examine how twenty-first-century representations of women slave-owning differ from pre-twenty-first-century texts, providing the field with a new lens to view these depictions in. It also focuses on "post" as a temporal, aesthetic, and theoretical argument.

This chapter provides a black feminist theoretical reading of Lara and Mistress Epps as well as a critique of how the white plantation mistress trope is represented in twenty-first-century films. Black feminist theory is concerned with how intersectionality shapes identity and representations of blackness, whiteness, and gender. I will use a black feminist theoretical lens to address the following questions: How are representations of female slave-owners on film aligned with postmodern conceptions of identity? How are female slave-owners represented as consumers who use products to shape/reshape their identity? Lara and Mistress Epps are treated as commodities who further the slave economy by participating in selling and objectifying slaves, which demonstrates their dual positioning in slavery. Postmodernism purports that identity is a destabilized category; individuals are allowed the freedom to reinvent their identity however they see fit, as identity is not essential or inherent. Thus, Lara and Mistress Epps attempt to forge identities dissimilar to how plantation mistresses were supposed to look and act. The way in which they try to reinvent themselves pushes against traditional conceptions of identity during slavery, which demonstrates how the writers are inserting postmodern conceptions of identity into narratives about slavery, meshing the past with the present. Although they interact with male slaves, the films focus on their treatment of women slaves and their reaction to their roles in the domestic sphere.

Both films push against the tradition of American films to characterize white plantation mistresses as delicate and naive. While non-American films, such as *Quilombo*, do not shy away from portraying white women slave-owners/mistresses as vicious, the literature review section of this chapter illustrates how American films are hesitant to grapple with white women's complicated role in slavery. This is dissimilar to American literature, in which, as demonstrated in the previous two chapters, the evil white plantation mistress is a prominent trope in texts such as *Our Nig*, *Incidents in the Life of a Slave Girl*, *Conquistadora*, and the literary version of *Twelve Years a Slave*. I argue that both films divorce white womanhood from its pure and noble connotations by showing the explicit ways Lara and Mistress Epps participate in the dehumanization of slaves.

The White Plantation Mistress on Screen

The white plantation mistress in American films is usually portrayed as spoiled, childish, and weak. Scarlett O'Hara is the basis of this stereotype—she "is often classified as a misrepresentation of antebellum southern women or the embodiment of white southern womanhood that has historically justified the oppression of African-Americans" (Scarlett O'Hara as Confederate Woman). However, some critics challenge this characterization of Scarlett and insist that she is a brave heroine. The goal of Margaret D. Bauer's *A Study of Scarletts: Scarlett O'Hara and Her Literary Daughters* is to rescue Scarlett from her critics, as she argues that Scarlett "is an inspiration to female readers, an icon in American popular culture, and yet she is more often than not condemned for being a sociopathic bitch" (12). She also argues that Scarlett's obtuseness and inability to run the plantation after her family begins dying off is a more realistic portrayal of white Southern women than Melanie's characterization, who, contrary to Scarlett, immediately begins helping the Confederate cause. In many ways, Scarlett fails to become an efficient slave-owner.

Julie Marsden, the protagonist of the 1938 film *Jezebel*, is often compared to Scarlett; similarly, she is characterized as evil and manipulative. In the film's most iconic scene, Julie wears a striking red dress to the Olympus ball instead of a white gown, which white women were expected to wear during this time period. Whiteness symbolizes purity, and Julie's refusal to adapt this color represents her tainted identity. As Michael Bibler argues, "These scenes thus code Julie's choice to wear the gown as an affront to aristocratic southern customs and the very codes of white femininity," which demonstrates Julie's failure to adjust to her role as a plantation mistress. After the yellow fever epidemic becomes more pronounced and starts killing more white men, Julie is tasked with controlling the plantation, as well as the slaves, but feels that she is unfit to do so. Unlike Scarlett, she does not interact with her slaves— even if Scarlett is yelling or hitting the slaves, she does acknowledge that they exist.

Scarlett O'Hara and Julie Marsden are the precursors for Blanche Maxwell, the white plantation mistress in *Mandingo* (1975) who is criticized by the other characters for being impure. On her wedding night, Hammond, her husband, is shocked to discover that she is not a virgin, which taints her reputation. After learning that her husband is having sex with slaves, Blanche forces Mede, a slave who participates in Mandingo fighting, to sleep with her and tells him that she will accuse him of rape if he disobeys her. After Blanche gives birth to a biracial baby, Hammond poisons her, which shows how unfaithful white women who do not fulfill their duties as plantation mistresses are punished with death.

In 1993, *Alex Haley's Queen: The Story of an American Family* becomes a television miniseries starring Halle Berry as the titular character. Queen is the product of an interracial romance between Easter and James Jackson, Jr., her slave-master. Easter is verbally and mentally abused by Lizzie Perkins, James's wife and mistress of the plantation who later treats Queen with the same disdain. After the Civil War begins, James enlists in the Confederate Army, leaving Lizzie in charge of the plantation. Slaves begin to leave the plantation and head north, stifling the crop production. In order to keep up with market demands, Lizzie works in the field, harvesting crops, until one of her neighbors insists that the field is no place for a plantation mistress. Lizzie is covered in dirt during this scene, suggesting that she is no longer pure, similar to how their choice of clothing marks Scarlett, Julie, and Blanche as impure. Lizzie cannot keep the plantation intact after Union soldiers destroy it, and she exemplifies the idea that plantation mistresses are failed owners who cannot run their property sufficiently.

As these films demonstrate, white plantation mistresses are depicted as being sexually impure rather than economically impure, and "had tacitly accepted their place within the South's gender and racial hierarchy, and. . . . were not socialized to fill the masculine roles of family head and business manager," which results in their failure as slave masters; however, the conceptualization of this trope changes in twenty-first-century representations (Antolini 26). The post-neo-slave narrative allows for this alteration—because gender identity is no longer conceived as a fixed concept, women are portrayed as fluctuating between being oppressed and oppressing others; therefore, contemporary representations of white plantation mistresses show how they have mastered the slave-owner role. Specifically, in *Django Unchained*, Calvin praises Lara's bartering skills, admiring her ability to sell female slaves.

12 Years a Slave and Mistress Epps

In *12 Years a Slave*, Solomon (Chiwetel Ejiofor) is a free man in New York, where he is a musician with a wife and children. Two men offer him a music gig but instead trick him into slavery. Due to the Fugitive Slave Act, black people in the North technically were not free, as they could be taken at any time and forced into slavery down south, which blurs the boundaries between the north and south, slavery and freedom. He is sold to William Ford (Benedict Cumberbatch), a white Christian slave-owner who reads bible sermons to his slaves. After tensions arise between Solomon and a few white male workers, Ford sells him to Master Epps (Michael Fassbender). There, he encounters Patsey (Lupita Nyong'o), a slave woman who routinely picks the most cotton and is the object of Master Epps's sadistic behavior. Mistress Epps (Sarah Paulson) abuses Patsey so badly that Patsey asks Solomon to mercy kill her. After several tumultuous years as Master Epps's slave, Solomon meets Bass (Brad Pitt), a Canadian freelance worker who gives Solomon's northern friends a note explaining his predicament. Eventually, Solomon returns to New York, but Patsey and the other slaves remain in captivity, demonstrating that slavery continues after the film ends.

Although scholars have analyzed Mistress Epps's vicious disposition, as well as her abusive treatment of Patsey, most do not focus on the subtle ways the film characterizes her subjugation. White plantation mistresses occupied a contradictory space in the domestic sphere in particular and slavery as a whole—some went so far as to compare their plight to slaves. Because of white women's subservience to their husbands, Mistress Epps does not have the power to rebel against Master Epps, which is why her anger is misplaced onto Patsey. She uses emasculating and vindictive language to show her disdain for him, such as insulting his manhood by calling him a "eunuch" and suggesting that he needs to beat his slaves before they plan a rebellion and kill them in their sleep. However, her attempts are insufficient, as Master Epps either ignores her or reminds her of her roots, "back to the hog's trough."

Mistress Epps, similar to Lara, looks down from the top floor of the white plantation to watch what the slaves are doing. The first scene featuring Mistress Epps occurs when she disdainfully observes Patsey humming and creating corn husk dolls. Patsey creates both white and brown dolls out of corn husks, and the white dolls resemble Mistress Epps's all-white dress and bonnet. This parallel characterizes Mistress Epps as a commodity—she is presented to the audience as a commodity who symbolizes leisure and the domestic sphere. She is a crop on the plantation who rebels against those who are lower in rank than her. Even in moments of leisure, whiteness is penetrating and omniscient. Whiteness as innocent and pure is also deconstructed. While some scholars, such as Stephanie Li, assess that this scene as an intrusion of Patsey's privacy, as well as whiteness as all-encompassing, for my literary project, I am interested in how this scene treats Mistress Epps as a commodity. It transforms her into a member of the slave economy as both a slaver and a victim.

Mistress Epps has a troubling relationship with Solomon, as she asks him to make financial transactions for her and demeans his speech patterns. When Solomon runs an errand for Mistress Epps, he mentions to slave catchers that he belongs to her, demonstrating the immense reputation and ubiquitous role she has within the slaver community even though she never actually leaves the plantation. Usually, the man is the master who runs the plantation and conducts business in the public sphere. This demonstrates the immense power her name and reputation has outside of the domestic sphere even if her power is overshadowed by her husband on the plantation. Her attempts to conduct financial transactions on the plantation, such as when she demands that Master Epps "sell the negress," (Patsey) fail, as her husband undermines her financial authority.

Mistress Epps is confined to the house during most of her scenes, and when she interacts with slaves, she is on the porch, above them, symbolizing her position on the pedestal. However, Mistress Epps's wardrobe changes now that she is no longer the "pure" woman on the pedestal. After she breaks up Master Epps and Solomon's fight, her dress looks stained, representing the duality of her position of plantation mistress. Her dress completely transforms from white to brown in the scene where she gives the other slaves food while refusing to feed Patsey. This scene demonstrates Mistress Epps's inability to act kind toward her slaves, as her act is still evil and heartless.

Her dress is also brown in the scene where she throws glass in Patsey's face. Patsey is wearing a pure white dress, a stark contrast to Mistress Epps's clothing, which represents a racial role reversal, as Patsey is the meek victim and Mistress Epps is the dark, evil owner. Mistress Epps's dress also resembles a rotten corn husk, showing that her character is now unredeemable damaged goods.

Black Women in *12 Years a Slave*

In *12 Years a Slave*, the black women characters receive more attention and sympathy than in the original narrative. This, I argue, is due to contemporary black feminist activists who demand more representations of black women's experiences. Tamara Winfrey Harris praises Steve McQueen for "a uniquely impressive job of illustrating female slave experiences through the women that Northup encounters during his years of bondage" but reminds us that *12 Years a Slave* is still told through Solomon's perspective. Harris's critique comes after *12 Years a Slave*'s release, but she expresses a frustrated sentiment that many black feminists share. bell hooks argues that "No other group in America has so had their identity socialized out of existence as have black women," chastising American culture for treating black men as the default faces of the black existence and rarely acknowledging black women's experiences when questions of gender are raised (*Ain't I a Woman* 7). hooks continues to argue that "Sexist historians and sociologists have provided the American public with a perspective on slavery in which the most cruel and dehumanizing impact of slavery in the lives of black people was that black men were stripped of their masculinity," which demonstrates how slaves' experiences are still gendered as male, pushing black women out of the frame.

It is possible that in response to black feminists' calls for more representations of slave women's experiences, McQueen and Ridley made a conscious decision to include more black women into the film, and the scenes where the film deviate from the narrative are when black women characters are illuminated. At the beginning of the film, while Solomon is packed inside a slave ship, a black woman crawls on top of him, guides his hand as he fingers her, and cries once she climaxes. In an interview with *The New York Times*, McQueen explains his rationale for including this scene: "Slaves are working all day. Their lives are owned, but those moments, they have to themselves. I just wanted a bit of tenderness—the idea of this woman reaching out for sexual healing in a way, to quote Marvin Gaye. She takes control of her own body. Then after she's climaxed, she's back where she was. She's back in hell, and that's when she turns and cries." This scene, for McQueen, exemplifies black female agency and allows a slave woman to have control over her pleasures and desires. Contrarily, Solomon is a passive recipient who does not move away from the woman or deny her advances. McQueen's explanation also represents a postmodern approach to using the present as a methodology for reading the past—he refers to this moment as "sexual healing," an homage to Marvin Gaye's famous song. This, I argue, is a crucial characteristic of the post-neo-slave narrative, which functions as a genre that allows artists to make contemporary interventions into representations of slavery, and this scene represents a response to contemporary black feminists' calls for more explorations of slave women's experiences.

This interpretation, however, is one that some critics have pushed against and instead argue that the emphasis on black women's pain is a source of "torture porn." Film critic Armond White criticizes the film for capitalizing on "an opportune moment when film culture—five years into the Obama administration—indulges stories about Black victimization" (*Huffington Post* review). Artist Kara Walker, whose silhouette art pieces have also been criticized for indulging in black exploitation, is disturbed by the many scenes that depict Patsey's abuse: "Staying on that scene and coming back to Patsey over and over, she is abused and deteriorating and wanting to die. We don't need to see that scene over and over again" (*NY Times* interview). I would complicate these interpretations by suggesting that making Patsey the focus on the film allows the audience to connect with her, and thus, makes them more sympathetic to slave women's experiences. Although I agree with many black feminist scholars who want more films that genuinely explore black women's experiences, *12 Years a Slave* effectively highlights the dismal treatment slave women received.

Another scene that has caused controversy involves Patsey—she asks Solomon to kill her because "I got no comfort in this life. If I can't buy mercy from yah, I'll beg it," which Solomon refuses to do. In the original narrative, Mistress Epps fails to use bribes to convince Solomon to kill Patsey:

> Nothing delighted the mistress so much as to see [Patsey] suffer, and more than once, when Epps had refused to sell her, has she tempted me with bribes to put her secretly to death, and bury her body in some lonely place in the margin of the swamp. Gladly would Patsey have appeased this unforgiving spirit, if it had been in her power, but not like Joseph, dared she escape from Master Epps, leaving her garment in his hand.

Noah Berlatsky argues that McQueen and Ridley misread this line, mistakenly attributing it to Patsey; however, when placed in a twenty-first-century context where black feminists are voicing their concerns about black women's visibility, this line exemplifies another postmodern intervention, rather than a misinterpretation. It was not uncommon for slaves to commit suicide rather than suffer through slavery. With the film 2010 adaptation of

Ntozake Shange's *For Colored Girls Who Have Considered Suicide/When the Rainbow Is Enuf* by Tyler Perry and Oprah Winfrey as well as the emergence of several organizations and blogs about health issues, black women's mental health is becoming a more visible and public conversation. McQueen, thus, connects these contemporary moments to history by illuminating how slaves used suicide as a way to assert their agency and size control of their lives. McQueen also imagines Patsey's interiority in a twenty-first-century context where that is allowed—as Li argues, "given the role of David Wilson, Northup's white amanuensis, in the text's production, such a request may have been excised as too disturbing for antebellum white readers," which demonstrates the shifting audiences as well as the limitations placed on the original narrative.

Mistress Shaw: Self-Exploiter

The postmodern interventions McQueen make all involve black women— while the sex scene with Solomon and Patsey's suicidal request scene both focus on black women asserting agency in a slave system that allows for none, Mistress Harriet Shaw's (Alfre Woodard) scene represents a contradictorily portrayal of a black woman slave-owner who uses her master's sexual advances as a method for avoiding "the end of a lash." Although Mistress Shaw is a character in the original narrative, she is only described as "the black wife of a white plantation owner" and has no dialogue. Mistress Shaw is a former black slave who marries her white slave-master, endowing her with a certain amount of control over the plantation. She has Sunday afternoon tea with Patsey on the porch of her plantation as Solomon runs up to her, telling her that Master Epps wants Patsey to come back. Mistress Epps strongly asserts herself as the master of the plantation when she silently orders a slave to refill her tea cup and calls Solomon "Nigger Platt," emphasizing the distance between her and the slaves. She addresses Solomon in the demeaning manner similar to how Master Epps does, a rhetorical strategy she uses to assert her authority. She tells Solomon to sit down and join them for tea as Solomon explains that Master Epps thinks Master Shaw is "something of a lothario and an unprincipled man." When Solomon calls Master Epps's words, "misguided," Mistress Shaw smiles and says, "No doubt . . . if not born outta truth itself." This shocks Solomon, who is surprised to hear Mistress Shaw refer to her husband in a derogatory fashion.

Mistress Shaw continues to bad-mouth her husband, even after she coyly waves to him as he attends to his horse:

> Ha! You worry for me? Got no cause to worry for my sensibilities. I ain't felt the end of a lash in 'mo years than I cain recall. Ain't worked a field, neither. Where

one time I served, now I got others servin' me. The cost to my current existence be Massa Shaw broadcasting his affections, 'n me enjoyin' his pantomime of fidelity. If that what keep me from the cotton pickin' niggers, that what it be. A small and reasonable price to be paid 'fo sure.

Mistress Shaw becomes an active participant in her own commodification. Like other representations of former slave women in this project, Mistress Shaw realizes the benefits of being a house slave when she describes how she "ain't worked a field." She discusses her predicament in terms of finances ("the cost to my current existence") as if she is pimping herself out to her husband. Simultaneously, she treats her husband as a piece of entertainment when she enjoys "his pantomime of fidelity," which suggests that this financial exchange is one where she gets to position herself as the gazer, rather than the one who is violated by the gaze. The film demonstrates how slaves were on call to entertain their masters during any time of day, and Mistress Shaw adapts the language and mannerisms of the planter class. Later, Mistress Shaw advises Patsey to "take comfort," in Master Epps's sexual violations, encouraging her to use the slave system to her advantage, for she may also end up as a plantation mistress rather than a field slave. Although Mistress Shaw enjoys Patsey's company, she demeans her during this exchange since Patsey is not only a field slave, but the most efficient slave on Epps's plantation; Mistress Shaw's relationship to the planter class, as well as her condescending language toward Solomon and Patsey, undermines this scene's attempts to show unity among black people.

In light of contemporary debates surrounding sex work, this postmodern intervention imagines that some slave women might have displayed agency by acting as madams who sold themselves in exchange for a less laborious position on the plantation. It also depicts black women as participating in the exploitation of slaves, which contradicts their usual characterization as victims during this time period. Most black feminists disagree with sex work as a form of empowerment and agency for black women. When discussing hip hop's influence on young black women, Sharpley-Whiting argues that "sexual freedom is illusory," especially when considering that the hip hop video vixen stereotype originates from the perception of black women as jezebels during slavery (66). Hopkinson and Moore, however, suggest that "sex workers mobilize their sexualities in the marketplace of desire for their own interests of access, opportunity, mobility, and fame," which claims that sex workers may wield some form of agency and choice (Miller-Young). The twenty-first-century debates surrounding black female sexuality is something that McQueen might have been attuned to, which may explain why Mistress Shaw's role highlights how black women may have used sex as a form of agency.

The "End" of Slavery?

When Solomon leaves the plantation, Patsey and Mistress Epps are the last images he sees, as Patsey faints and Mistress Epps becomes a blur. This represents slavery's continuity even after Solomon is gone, which is a different ending than *Django Unchained*, where Django kills his enemies, burns the plantation, and rides off with Broomhilda. Broomhilda is armed with a rifle, which suggests that her resistance will continue off screen. Patsey's image is blurred as she lets out a heavy groan before she faints, as if she just saw a ghost, and another female slave rushes to her. Mistress Epps, however, keeps her attention on Solomon and is not fazed by Patsey's fainting—these are the images of slavery that the audience is supposed to embed in their brains after the film is over, snapshots of women's complex roles during slavery as well as the perception that slavery continues even when the screen fades to black, which is something that most American films do not grapple with. Mistress Epps's blurring fades into the road, representing another example of her characterization as a commodity and piece of property.

Lara Lee: "Tonic to Tired Eyes"

Lara Lee Candie-Fitzwilly is Calvin Candie's widowed sister who acts as the mistress of the infamous Candyland plantation where Broomhilda is captured. We are first introduced to the Candyland plantation when a wide angle lens shows the white plantation and its yellow cornfields while Django, Schultz, Calvin, and a group of slaves ride down the path leading to it—the song that plays in the background ("Nicaragua" [feat. Pat Metheny] by Jerry Goldsmith) makes it seem as if they are participating in a parade. Lara is drinking tea with a gentleman while Cora, her female slave, stands on the side. At this point, we do not see her face and only see the back of her. The flowers in her hair and the pink dress makes her seem younger than she actually is, as if she is a princess at a tea party. She stops drinking her tea and smiles as she sees them riding in, and we now see that Lara is in her forties, which is older than her initial princess image suggests. This princess image is one that is slowly deconstructed as the film progresses.

Though the audience has already seen Lara at her tea party, she is introduced after Calvin dramatically screams, "Where is my beautiful sister?" She emerges from the plantation with a pink dress that is decorated in flowers. This scene presents Lara as both a commodity and an owner, which demonstrates her precarious position as a plantation mistress. She walks out of the plantation slowly, with Cora behind her, and poses for the audience, as if she is in a beauty pageant. Calvin introduces Lara to Schultz as his widowed sister, an "attractive Southern belle." This scene demonstrates her duality as a sister and lover—her body language with Calvin suggests that their relationship is incestuous, as he kisses her frequently and gushes over her good looks, while he still wants Shultz to see her as an object of affection, which would solidify their brotherhood bond.[3] Calvin's emphasis on her status as a widow demonstrates that she is on the market as a hot commodity. This scene presents Lara as an object of affection as well as a slave-owner. She is placed on a pedestal until Schultz asks for Broomhilda, which sours Lara's mood and shows that she is not the object of his desires. Her face changes from happy to worried/disappointed: as Ortiz suggests, Lara is "gazing on Broomhilda," which "betrays in succession envy, desire, hate." Lara is the primary slave-owner when Calvin is away, as there are also some aspects of this scene that suggests how Lara had control of the plantation while Calvin was gone and was the one responsible for putting Broomhilda in the hot box.

In addition, Lara is further treated as a commodity and symbolizes a rose that Calvin gives to Dr. Schultz as a symbol of marriage offering, which is why she is decorated in flowers. Marriage is constructed as an alliance between families during this time period. Calvin deconstructs Lara's broken status as a widow by calling her "tonic to tired eyes" and drawing attention to her good looks. Wood discusses the significance of mourning wear, especially when widows entered the public sphere:

> Deep mourning ensured that women would remain identifiable as bereaved wives even after many years of husbandless legal independence. This visibility had mixed implications for slaveholding widows. Widow's weeds announced that a woman had no husband to protect her, so mourning may have made her more vulnerable to insult or manipulation at the hands of strangers. At the same time, black clothing silently explained why a widow entered into banks, courthouses, and other places of business where women rarely appeared. Mourning wear also contributed to widows' self-representation as ladies. (36)

Lara is clearly not in mourning gear—it is quite the opposite as her gown is cheerful and festive, which suggests a rejection of the societal responsibilities placed on widows. This is a postmodern construction of widowhood—the twenty-first-century widow does not wear black and is instead back on the market, flowers in tow, in search of a new husband.

Since "widows attached particular importance to the successful performance of domestic, archetypically feminine, labors," Lara's job as a plantation mistress is to keep the female slaves in line and ensure that the domestic sphere is tidy, hence why Calvin tasks her with cleaning up Broomhilda after removing her from the hot box so she can meet Schultz. Broomhilda needs to look flawless for her meeting with Schultz. Lara acts as a madam when she escorts Broomhilda up to Schultz's room so she can fulfill her duties as a comfort slave girl. When Schultz opens the door, we see a single frame of Lara, which makes it seem as if she came up to his room alone. This is another red herring—Lara is set up as the object of affection, as if she is the one on the pedestal, when it is Broomhilda who Schultz is after. This scene also demonstrates Lara's active participation in slavery—Broomhilda did not have a choice and was forced to enter Dr. Schultz's bedroom, her worried face showing that she was not comfortable with this transaction. Lara is content with pimping slave women out to white men, which challenges the idea that white women were innocent, inactive participants in slavery. Lara's objection to Calvin and Stephen showcasing Broomhilda's whip lashes on her back during dinner shows how much she cares about the appearance of the domestic space. Lara, by extension, looks bad if Broomhilda does, as if she cannot keep her slaves in line. This demonstrates that Lara's objection is more about her selfish need to keep up with appearances than stopping Broomhilda's humiliation, as the upkeep of clothing is constructed as a feminine task (46).

Although scholars credit Stephen for outing Django and Broomhilda, it is actually Lara who first alerts the dinner table that these two have chemistry. After flashing an envious eye at Broomhilda, who Schultz pretends to be smitten with, she mentions that Broomhilda "has eyes for Django," which makes Stephen question their motives. This innocent comment is the catalyst for the rest of the film, as the charade is now uncovered, which leads to her brother's death, and it further aligns Lara with the villains. Before Calvin confronts Schultz and Django, he tells Lara to speak with a slaver outside who is interested in buying female slaves since Lara knows more about slave women than he does, which illustrated how Lara is actively involved in the purchasing of slaves as well as highlights her mastery as a slave-owner. This deconstructs the characterization of white plantation mistresses as naïve and delicate, as Lara is just as guilty as her brother in furthering the slave economy. It also demonstrates Lara's skills as a plantation owner and mastery of bartering with slavers. When Django is captured after unsuccessfully attempting to rebel, Lara sells him to the Mining Company, which is reminiscent of how plantation mistresses handled slaves when their husbands died, and represents another example of how she barters with slavers.[4]

Although Lara's death has caused controversy among scholars, as some do not feel she deserved to die, it is quite clear why Django kills her since she participates in the exploitation and dehumanization of slaves throughout the film. Jarrod Dunham is surprised by Lara's murder, rationalizing that Django

> quite literally shoots every White person he encounters, including Miss Laura, the relatively sympathetic sister of Candie, whose principal role in the film has been to insist on the indecency of displaying Hildi's lash scars for the dinner guests. It would seem that Django is violently enacting an absolutist rebellion

against slavery, taking vengeance against every White representative of the institution he encounters. However, while the pretense of radical justice remains intact, Django's flippant murder of Miss Laura, whose complicity in the slave economy is not obviously greater than that of Schultz, his late owner and master, suggests there is something indiscriminate in his violence—or, rather, that he is discriminating on the basis of race, and not guilt.

I would argue the opposite—Lara is implicated in furthering the slave economy—she acts as a madam when she escorts Broomhilda to Schultz's room as well as negotiates with slavers, which demonstrates her guiltiness. When considering these acts, Lara's murder is justified, as she is an active participant in keeping slave culture afloat, and she is not murdered based on just her race, but on the guilty acts she commits.

In the midst of Django's brutal and bloody revenge, he murders Lara with a single shot to the abdomen, and she flies out of the scene in a cartoonish, fantastical manner, which is different than the serious way other white people are murdered. For Michael Ralph, Tarantino is forced to construct Lara's murder in this fashion, calling this "a cinematic technique to lessen, for the audience, the moral weight of having a menacing black man kill a delicate white woman" (410). When placed in a "post-racial", twenty-first-century American context, this suggests that there are still politics and limitations to Django's revenge, as the black male predator who targets innocent white women trope is popular in American films.[5] This would complicate Django's characterization as the "black male hero" Tarantino wants audiences to visualize him as. I would push against Ralph's analysis, as the film challenges the construction of Lara as "delicate," and purports that her death is justified. Another aspect of the film that complicates Ralph's analysis is Django's killing of a white woman earlier in the film. He murders a female slaver, played by Zoe Bell, who views images through her stereoscope and works for Stonesipher as a slave tracker. When discussing acts of seeing in the film, William Brown observes how "spectacle (bodies as attractions that one looks at in a supposedly detached manner) is key to capitalism and slavery," implicating the female slaver for her consumption of slavery imagery for both pleasure and research, which to Django, is a form of guilt, hence why he unapologetically murders her, along with her seven coworkers. I argue that the film attempts to disrupt the plantation mistress on a pedestal trope by killing both Lara and the unnamed white woman slaver. *Django Unchained* and *12 Years a Slave* implicate white women for their role in slavery, something that most American slave movies refuse to do. Postmodernity allows for these interventions since white plantation mistresses are characterized as commodities who commodify slaves. Thus, white womanhood is deconstructed, providing infinite possibilities for constructions of white women characters.

RESCUING BROOMHILDA: WOMEN
AS COMMODITIES

Django Unchained starts with Dr. King Schultz (Christopher Waltz), a German dentist who now works as a bounty hunter, purchasing Django Freeman (Jamie Foxx) from the Speck Brothers. The two begin an apprentice-expert relationship where Schultz trains Django as a gunslinger who kills people with bounties on them. After Schultz frees him, Django asks Schultz to help him locate his wife, Broomhilda (Kerry Washington), as they were separated when they both tried to escape slavery. They learn that Broomhilda is held captive at the Candyland plantation, which is owned by Calvin Candie (Leonardo DiCaprio), and Schultz devises a complicated plan in order to free her. Django and Schultz fool Calvin into thinking they are interested in purchasing Mandingo fighters, and Calvin invites him to Candyland. This is where they encounter Stephen (Samuel L. Jackson), an old house slave who acts as if he is the true owner of the plantation, and Lara Lee Candie-Fitzwilly (Laura Cayouette), Calvin's widowed sister. Schultz pretends as if he is interested in a romantic encounter with Broomhilda, and when she enters his room, Schultz tells her in German that he and Django are there to rescue her. At dinner, Lara and Stephen uncover their charade, and Schultz kills Calvin. Schultz is then murdered by one of Calvin's henchmen, and Django steals a gun and goes on a murdering rampage. Eventually, Django and Broomhilda are reunited, and Django kills Stephen and all the white people on the plantation.

The purpose of my literary analysis is to highlight the women characters in *Django Unchained* and analyze their construction as commodities in the slave economy. Broomhilda, the primary female character and damsel in distress, is treated as an object by other characters, even by her own husband, Django, whose mission is to rescue her from the evil Candyland plantation. When Django is on his horse riding to Candyland, he sees an image of Broomhilda smiling and laughing in the cornfields. The yellow dress she wears blends into the tall corn stalks we see throughout the film, demonstrating that she is a crop, a commodity. This is a common construction of women in both films, as Lara is likened to a flower and Mistress Epps is juxtaposed against a white corn husk doll that Patsey creates. Osumare parallels Broomhilda's dress with Oshun the Yoruba goddess, who is also depicted as wearing a yellow, flowing dress, to champion Tarantino for invoking, "another parallel with African undertones through the meaning of Hildy's character" (83). This furthers my analysis by demonstrating how Broomhilda is a royal commodity in Django's eyes, as Africans' status in Africa (or among themselves) had little influence on whether or not they were enslaved. This also elevates the perception that

Broomhilda is different from other slaves, which is why she is worthy of rescuing in the first place.

Broomhilda is constructed as damaged goods by Calvin, who insists that she is not worth more than $300 due to being an escape risk and her battered back. Though the entire film focuses on Django's retribution, Broomhilda's resistance takes place off screen—she is initially separated from Django because of her attempts to escape and is later thrown naked in the hot box on the orders of Lara and Stephen for attempting to run away from Candyland—which stifles her character, as she never transcends her objectification. Women slaves commonly rebelled against their masters and tried to escape, as highlighted by Angela Davis and Deborah McDowell, but this is not the point of *Django Unchained*, as the film is more concerned with fraternal bonds and exploring the male hero figure in a spaghetti Western/antebellum slavery context.

Though a black woman being constructed as an object is not revolutionary or surprising, Broomhilda as a damsel in distress is, as black women are usually not characterized as worthy of support and rescuing. I would like to extend Halifu Osumare's analysis of Broomhilda as a damsel to suggest that she is occupying a space that black women are not allowed to enter. The damsel in distress is a common American cultural trope that focuses on the rescuing of vulnerable white women, from films such as *King Kong* to "Missing White Woman Syndrome," which is different from how kidnapped black women are constructed. As Sojourner Truth reminds us in her famous "Ain't I a Woman" speech, black women were treated as workhorses who labored alongside black men and did not have the same feminist narrative trajectory as white women, who were fighting for the right to work and exit the domestic sphere. This leads to the characterization of black women as mules, as Zora Neale Hurston aptly suggests. bell hooks describes how "black women fantasize about not working" and "dream of being able to stop working for a time if there is a man to watch their back," which demonstrates that some black women, even black feminist scholars who are concerned with gender equality, are receptive of being a damsel in distress because they are usually not portrayed this way. While many scholars, such as Dana Weber and Robert von Dassanowsky, have drawn a connection between the Brunhilde German tale and discussed the damsel in distress trope, most have not considered how being a black woman complicates Broomhilda's characterization as a damsel, especially in a slavery context where black women were blamed for their subjugation As Houston Baker explains, "In slave law black women are seductresses, deemed so lascivious by nature and so passionate in lust for carnality that they are always dangerously willing to give themselves to lust. They are thus legally incapable of being "raped" (33). Because slave women are considered property, their subjectivity and citizenship is flattened, which makes them the opposite of damsels.

Broomhilda as a damsel in distress is complicated, however, by her characterization as an atypical black woman. Django emphasizes that Broomhilda is different from other slaves, as she speaks German and is attractive enough to serve as a "comfort slave." Comfort slaves are treated like prostitutes—they provide sexual services to buyers. The money goes to the owner, not to the slave. Despite a large body of research[6] that suggests that slaves' reliance on community as a form of resistance and support was a crucial element of slavery, Django and Broomhilda do not show any communal bonds with their fellow slaves—in some instances, Django is even antagonistic or condescending toward them.[7] Django does "next to nothing to free the rest of the slaves," which emphasizes his disconnect from the rest of the slave community (28). Perhaps Broomhilda is allowed characterization as a damsel because she is different from other slave women, hence why she is worth saving.

Ishmael Reed dismisses Broomhilda as "the usual sexual toy role assigned to minority actresses by Hollywood," speaking to the stereotype of black women as Jezebels. While his assessment is accurate, especially when we consider Kerry Washington's role as Olivia Pope on *Scandal*, it is important to place Broomhilda in a slavery context where black women were treated as sex objects and raped by their masters. This illuminates Lara's role as a madam who pimps Broomhilda out to Schultz, as she is helping further the exploitive transaction between white male slave-owners and black women slaves.

The New Plantation Mistress

12 Years a Slave and *Django Unchained*'s depictions of plantation mistresses differ from the traditional Hollywood narrative by illuminating their mastery of slave-ownership and challenging their characterization as innocent and naive. The women characters understand the dynamics of slavery and seek to increase their positioning within the plantation hierarchy. Both films complicate the racial and gender conventions associated with slave-owners by showing representation of black women slave-owners who participate in their own self-exploitation. The next chapter will focus on the plantation mistress trope in hip hop music and analyze how black women rappers utilize both slave and slave-owning language to construct their identity as liberators and colonizers.

NOTES

1. While *12 Years a Slave* takes place in New York, Washington, DC, and New Orleans, it is not strictly a white or American production. Several actors, including Lupita N'yongo, Chiwetel Ejiofor, and Michael Fassbender are not American. Steve McQueen, the director, is black and British. Although this is not the focus on my project, one can argue that this makes the film a transatlantic, rather than American, production.

2. For more debates about humor as a subversive strategy in slavery representations, see Brandon J. Manning's chapter "Laughing to Keep from Crying: Dave Chapelle's Self-Exploration with 'The Nigger Pixie'" in *The Psychic Hold of Slavery: Legacies in American Expressive Culture*.

3. Due to Calvin's overt affection toward his sister, as well as his flamboyant personality, some scholars read him as queer and argue that *Django Unchained* is a battle between different forms of masculinities (see Catherine Keyser's "The Sweet Tooth of Slavery: *Django Unchained* and Kara Walker's *A Subtlety*"). Django and Schultz represent the masculine gunslingers while Calvin is characterized as a feminine party host that never had to work for anything. These seemingly opposite representations are mitigated by their mutual interests in slave-owning and Mandingo fighting.

4. This is similar to how in *Beloved*, Mrs. Garner sold Sethe and the other slaves to Schoolteacher.

5. Examples include *Animal House*, *Predator*, *King Kong*, etc. In some films, particularly science fiction ones, the villain is racialized as a black man even if he is not supposed to be human.

6. See Deborah White's *Ar'n't I a Woman?: Female Slaves in the Plantation South*, Charles Joyner's *Down by the Riverside: A South Carolina Slave Community*, and John Blassingame's *The Slave Community: Plantation Life in the Antebellum South*.

7. Though one could argue that he had to play this role in order to convince Calvin that he was a serious slaver. At the same time, Dr. Schultz warns Django that he's being too harsh on the slaves and needs to tone it down, demonstrating that his slaver persona is too strong and dramatic.

Chapter 4

"The Rap Purist"

The Plantation Mistress
in Hip Hop Music

Since its conception in the Bronx during the 1970s, hip hop lyrics have always contained references to slavery, as well as the continent of Africa. "The Message" by Grandmaster Flash and the Furious utilizes "the jungle" metaphor, which became a repetitive image throughout the genre, and draws parallels between inner city environments and the concept of African jungles. Kunta Kinte, the main character of Alex Haley's *Roots*, is referenced by many rappers, including Lil' Wayne, Kendrick Lamar, and Missy Elliot, which I will discuss later in this chapter. Due to its roots as an African American genre, hip hop's connection to slavery is apparent since African American identity, and American identity in general, is heavily connected to the United States' slavery history. Hip hop culture is interested in the slavery traumas that helped create the African American identity and experience.

Although many scholars have explored hip hop's connection to slavery, there is not as much scholarship about how female rappers utilize antebellum slave-owning metaphors and imagery in their music. The language of ownership is rampant in hip hop—when an MC wins a rap battle, it is often referred to as "owning" one's opponent. Female rappers are meshing ownership metaphors with slavery language, which adds another dimension to the language of ownership. To own an opponent in a rap battle is to demonstrate mastery over them and show that the victor is the superior rapper. In a slavery context, this ownership extends beyond linguistic victory and shows how the winner owns the loser's entire persona, similar to how slave-owners renamed their slaves, sold them on command, and bred them whenever they saw fit. When Nicki Minaj claims in "Did It On Em" that "all these bitches are my sons/I'm gonna get some bibs for them," she emphasizes that she gave birth to other rappers' personas since they are copying off of her. Their version of

Nicki Minaj is juvenile and sloppy, similar to a baby, and she denies these rappers authenticity and ownership over their personas. Rah Digga and Missy Elliott, the stars of this chapter, are doing something similar while adding slavery imagery to their conception of ownership.

Bernard Bell and Ashraf H.A. Rushdy's original conception of a neo-slave narrative focuses on an enslaved literary character's journey from bondage to freedom with the purpose of debunking romanticized representations of slavery that often exclude black people's experiences; however, this definition is challenged by postmodern notions of identity as well as the emergence of slavery imagery in non-literary genres such as hip hop music, therefore, we need a new term to describe the different articulations of this new subgenre—the "post-neo-slave narrative." I define the post-neo-slave narrative as a genre consisting of literary and non-literary texts that allows for the incorporation of postmodernist theories within the neo-slave narrative. The music lyrics included of Digga and Elliot exemplify how twenty-first-century genres such as hip hop music contain an alternative, postmodern perspective on issues of race, civil rights, and slavery that differs from the civil rights era texts Bell and Rushdy analyze. Currently, the postmodern slave narrative and the neo-slave narrative are discussed in opposition, and my project demonstrates the importance of blending the genres to create the post-neo-slave-narrative. The original conception of the postmodern slave narrative focuses on how literary artists, such as Toni Morrison, Ishmael Reed, and Charles Johnson, use fantastical elements to engage with slavery's monstrosities, which A Timothy Spaulding argues is a departure from the neo-slave narrative, where realistic representations of slavery that mirror slave narratives are championed. Rather than choose between the fantastical postmodern slave narrative and the realist neo-slave narrative, the texts that I examine in this project are using conventions of both genres to demonstrate how contemporary inequalities are rooted in slavery practices.

BLACK FEMALE RAPPERS, HIP HOP MUSIC, AND THE SLAVE-OWNING TROPE

The slave-owning trope draws a direct link between the past and the present with the user imagining how ownership transforms their present experience into a material entity of slavery. The slave-owning trope gestures toward symbolic registers of slave owning (the master's whip, writing utensils, papers, plantations, tight spaces, chains, etc.) to help the person using it understand their millennial experiences of the oppressed/oppressor binary. The slave-owning trope is a tool that women rappers utilize to exploit the contradictions that surround traditional conventions of postmodern identity. In her study of postmodern identity and its relationship to fashion imagery, Elena Abrudan highlights these contradictions when she discusses how postmodern identity "is a construct that requires a constant process of innovation and renewal taking into consideration the evolution of society" while observing that consumers are "asked to feel free to make a choice, to be themselves, according to the principles of democratic society; at the same time, it is supposed that a consumer must be similar to many other individuals that will acquire and consume the products that correspond to the esthetic, quality and functionality norms of the times" (4). In other words, postmodern identity purports that people are allowed to freely construct their identities as long as that identity is replicable, readable, and marketable.

Black women rappers are often marketable and readable to the general American public if they portray a hyper-sexualized aesthetic that replicates black stereotypes. Missy Elliott and Rah Digga, the case studies for this chapter, are challenging these stereotypes by using the slave-owning trope as a tool to prove their lyrical dominance and draw connections between millennial culture and antebellum slavery. While their lyrics champion freedom and independence, Elliott and Digga have appropriated antebellum slave-owning language with the goal of proving that their competitors should be subservient to them. Black women rappers frequently reference slavery in their lyrics[1]; however, their references to slavery move beyond their position as helpless victims. When most rappers draw parallels between slavery and millennial issues of inequality, they emphasize their status as oppressed people, but some women rappers are, contradictorily, resisting and reinforcing this dichotomy. Black women rappers do not literally own slaves but are rather discussing their power in a metaphorical sense. This metaphorical power is often discussed materially by evoking symbolic registers of slavery.

While some black feminist scholars resist using symbolic registers to connect the contemporary black experience to slavery, I argue that these symbols acclimated to contemporary America in harmful ways, which is why it is important to critique and challenge them. "Black women," Joan Morgan writes, "can no more be defined by the cumulative sum of our pain than blackness can be defined solely by the transgenerational atrocities delivered at the hands of American racism. Because black folks are more than the stench of the slave ship, the bite of the dogs, or the smoldering of freshly lynched flesh" (6). Morgan rejects the use of slavery symbolic registers such as the slave ship to define black Americans and does not want the black experience defined by oppression and negativity; however, I argue that these symbols are crucial to understanding the link between slavery and the present. As many rappers remind us, the symbols of slavery acclimated to contemporary America in harmful ways. They serve as metaphorical tools for understanding the racism black people endured. The chains used to bind, capture, and torture slaves transformed into the flashy chains we see rappers wear today. In M.O.P.'s "Ante Up," they draw a strong connection between economic oppression and slavery, arguing that rappers are becoming slaves to material chains.

Although demonstrating how these symbols serve as tools of oppression is a valuable practice, this chapter is more interested in exploring how black female rappers use these symbols as tools of power. Similar to their constructed identities as metaphoric slave-owners, Rah Digga and Missy Elliott have a complex relationship with slavery symbols that simultaneously demonstrates their subjugation and methods used to oppress others; hence why the slave-owning trope is a useful concept for understanding their usage of slavery imagery.

Black Feminism, Postmodernism, and Slave-Owning

Using scholarship by Barbara Christian, Melissa Harris-Perry, and Patricia Hill Collins to construct my argument, this chapter provides a black feminist critique of postmodern identity and conceptualizations of ownership. The first aspect of my argument focuses on the connection between postmodernism and black women rappers' lyrical slave-owning of their opponents. As scholars such as Judith Butler, Brian Ott, Elena Abrudan, and Jean Baudrillard have demonstrated, postmodern identity is based on the idea that identity is not fixed and instead fluctuates. It challenges essentialist theories of identity that were championed by some modernists. Postmodernism has also changed conceptions of metaphoric slave ownership by demonstrating how identity is fluid; while, similar to characters in neo-slave narratives, black women rappers speak of a metaphoric journey from bondage to freedom in their lyrics, they also brag about their ability to enslave their "haters," which illustrates the power and domination they wield over others as well as challenges the perception that hip hop is a masculine space that women cannot thrive in.

I also argue that black women rappers are easing the tension between black feminist theory and postmodern identity. While Patricia Hill Collins praises how postmodernism "rejects notions of epistemological and methodological certainty provided by the natural sciences, social sciences, and other discourses of modernity that have been used to justify Black women's oppression" (124), she is weary of its ability to empower black women, arguing that "deconstructive methodologies operate more effectively as a critique of power than as a theory of empowerment" (8). In response to Collins's statement, I argue that black women rappers are using conventions of postmodern identity as both a tool of empowerment and critique of power as well as re-conceptualizing representations of slave-owning.

In post-neo-slave narratives, black women rappers use the slave-owning trope to assert their dominance and power over others. Simultaneously, their lyrics serve as a space to highlight their oppressions. Neo-slave narratives focus on how black slaves were oppressed but not necessarily on how they oppressed others. The notion of postmodern identity has changed the original neo-slave narrative conception, as women slave-owners' identity fluctuates between oppressed and oppressor. Black women rappers are using this trope to challenge the masculine climate of hip hop as well as comment on twenty-first-century inequalities that black Americans face.

The next aspect of my argument discusses how black women rappers employ the slave-owning trope to complicate the white plantation mistress trope that is prevalent in American culture. Writers often portray white women slave-owners/plantation mistresses as evil agents of the slave system who enforce, rather than challenge, slavery.[2] These representations are usually stereotypical and do not show how complex white women slave-owners/plantation mistresses are. By using the slave-owning trope, which is steeped in antebellum slavery imagery, black women rappers are simultaneously challenging and enforcing slavery, which demonstrates how complicated their relationship to slave culture is. As a result, they are providing a new and alternative conception of the white women slave-owner/plantation mistress trope.

Black women rappers compare the contemporary struggles they face to the slave experience by drawing a parallel between their oppressions. Scholars such as Michelle Alexander and Saidiya Hartman have argued that slavery has not disappeared but has rather transformed into disguised forms of discrimination such as the war on drugs, the prison industrial complex, and redlining. While I agree with the assessment that slavery has transformed rather than disappeared, it's worth questioning what happens to the concept of slave-ownership. Has the definition and criteria for slave-owners also shifted? Rappers have characterized the police and the music industry as akin to slave-owners—these are hegemonic institutions that exploit and marginalize black people. While this is an accurate description of these institutions, some black people are complacent participants in this marginalization, and I am fascinated by how black women rappers reify the very institutional forces they are fighting against. Black women rappers use slave imagery to flirt with the idea of being a slave-owner that has complete domination over others, and scholarship does not explore their characterization as slave owners thoroughly enough. As a result, this chapter provides a much needed intervention that includes women into the scholarly conversation surrounding slave ownership and hip hop.

THE SLAVE-OWNING TROPE AS A METHOD
USED TO CRITIQUE HIP HOP CULTURE

Crass. Aggressive. Misogynistic. Critics use these harsh adjectives to describe hip hop as a genre of music. Many black feminist scholars, such as Joan Morgan, Tricia Rose, Gwendolyn Pough, and Patricia Hill Collins, have debated about women's potential to possess power in a genre that is hostile toward them. "Hip hop," Gwendolyn Pough argues, "gendered as feminine has no agency. She is something men rappers love, something they do. She does not act; she is acted upon" (94). Pough's analysis questions how black women rappers can thrive in a genre characterized as feminine and passive. Murray Forman, however, believes that black women rappers can use hip hop music as one of the "new forums . . . through which to voice their joys and passions as well as their outrage against prevailing hierarchal structures of domination" (41). Furthermore, Forman asserts that black women rappers used hip hop music to "generate their own discourse of empowerment" (45). Tricia Rose agrees with Forman's assertions as she emphasizes the importance of "women who challenge sexism expressed by male rappers, yet sustain dialogue with them, who reject the racially coded aesthetic hierarchies in American popular culture by privileging black women bodies, and who support black women's voices and history" (182). Rose and Forman published their texts in 1994; although "raunchy" women rappers existed during that time, does their assessment remain accurate when we discuss sexually suggestive black women rappers such as Lil' Kim[3] and Nicki Minaj in a new millennium context?[4] If we assume that hip hop is a masculine space, what methods have black women rappers used to penetrate this space, to bring black women's issues to the forefront?

I propose that the slave-owning trope is an example of how black women rappers assert agency in a male-dominated space while simultaneously drawing attention to the racial, sexual, and gender discrimination they face within the hip hop industry. The slave-owning trope turns traditional places of oppression into spaces of power. This trope helps black women rappers re-construe the white plantation mistress trope to draw attention to the dismal treatment of women in slave culture while also demonstrating the power they wield. The Southern white plantation mistress, who Paula Giddings describes as "enmeshed in an interracial web in which wives, children, and slaves were all expected to obey the patriarchal head of household," transforms into an empowered black women rapper when placed into a hip hop context (43).

"Girls, Girls, Get That Cash"

Antebellum Slavery, Hip Hop, and Black Female Objectification

Before I begin close reading Rah Digga's "Harriet Thugman" and Missy Elliott's "Work It," I want to provide background information about hip hop as a music genre and why rappers are inclined to use slavery imagery to describe their oppression. This section will also highlight the politics behind the economization and commodification of hip hop. In *Check It While I Wreck It: Black Womanhood, Hip-Hop Culture, and the Public Sphere*, Gwendolyn D. Pough uses Jurgen Habermas's theories of the public sphere as a backdrop for arguing that hip hop forced black people to enter the public sphere and maintain a strong presence: "Bringing wreck," Pough argues, "for Black participants in the public sphere historically, has meant reshaping the public gaze in such a way as to be recognized as human beings—as functioning and worthwhile members of society—and not to be shut out of or pushed away from the public sphere" (17). Black participants used the four elements of hip hop, graffiti writing, rapping, DJ-ing, and break dancing, as artistic expressions to accomplish this. This is similar to how former slaves used mastering Standard Written English as their gateway into the public sphere and as a method for convincing white abolitionists to fight for slaves' freedom. Slave narratives contained letters of endorsement from white abolitionists who attested to the slaves' writing skills and authenticity of their experiences. Like slave narratives, hip hop became corporatized. Patrick T.J. Browne outlined abolitionist William Lloyd Garrison and Frederick Douglass's famous disagreement over Douglass's creation of *The North Star*, a newspaper that served as a competitor to Garrison's *Liberator*. Like hip hop, where many music labels and sponsors are owned by white people, abolitionism became a corporate entity that white abolitionists profited from by exploiting the black experience. The parallels between slaves' experiences and rappers' millennial experiences form the basis of my argument calling for scholars to read rap songs as post-neo-slave narratives.

In addition to exploring these parallels, this chapter is also interested in how the exploitation of the black women body in hip hop culture is reminiscent of their dismal treatment during antebellum slavery. Three stereotypes of black women emerged during slavery and the reconstruction era: the mammy, the sapphire, and the jezebel. Carolyn West describes how black women slaves were raped by their white male masters and connected this to the sexual assault they were subjected to during KKK raids. "The Jezebel stereotype," West writes, "which branded Black women as sexually promiscuous and immoral, was used to rationalize these sexual atrocities. This image gave the impression that Black women could not be rape victims because they always desired sex" (294). The jezebel stereotype characterizes black women as sexually promiscuous and available. The jezebel's sexuality is aggressive and characterized as a threat to American culture. Melissa Harris-Perry analyzes the connection between the Jezebel stereotype and the Welfare Queen stereotype when discussing a focus group she conducts where she talks with study participants about stereotypes of black women. She makes two lists—a list of myths and a list of facts—and asks the participants to place specific stereotypes of black women into one of those lists. Several participants agree that the Welfare Queen stereotype is rooted in fact: "There are a lot of black women out here living on the system," says one participant (34). The Welfare Queen stereotype exists because black women are perceived as sexually uncontrollable and constantly having babies out of wedlock, which relates back to the Jezebel stereotype.[5] The government marketed this stereotype to Americans through "The Moynihan Report,"[6] which characterized black women as socially deviant and lazy.

As opposed to the jezebel, the mammy stereotype renders black women as sexless and undesirable. Barbara Christian describes the mammy as "black in color as well as race and fat with enormous breasts that are full enough to nourish all children in the world; her head is perpetually covered with her trademark handkerchief to hide the kinky hair that marks her as ugly" (12–13). The sapphire stereotype describes black women as angry, confrontational, and intimidating. Black women slaves, as West writes, were "characterized as strong, masculinized workhorses who labored with Black men in the field or as aggressive women who drove their children and partners away with their overbearing natures" (295). This image manifests itself into the contemporary "Angry Black Women" stereotype.

The jezebel, mammy, and sapphire stereotypes are entrenched in hip hop music and form the basis for the misogynistic characterization of black women in this genre of music. Terry M. Adams and Douglas B. Fuller observe how the jezebel stereotype in hip hop manifests itself into the "ho," "video vixen," or "gold-digger" while the sapphire stereotype is akin to the "bitch" label (948). Heavyset black women rappers are often described as mammies by critics: in an article featured in *The New Yorker*, Hilton Als quotes Whitney Museum curator Thelma Golden who calls Missy Elliott a "cyber mammy" (Als). Whether or not black women rappers can subvert these three images is subject to debate. In her analysis of the 2001 version of Patti Labelle's "Lady Marmalade" performed by singers Mya, Pink, and Christina Aguilera and rappers Lil Kim and Missy Elliott, Imani Perry critiques Lil' Kim's "Pamela Anderson in brown skin" aesthetic by arguing that her pornographic gestures are no longer a method of subversion (141). Akin to the mammy persona, Missy Elliott appears in the music video not as a sex object but as "narrator/madam" who is "free from objectification" (145). I would classify Elliott as a stylish mammy—although she raps about her sexuality and toward the end of her career began to dress and dance more provocatively, she is rarely presented as a sex object in music videos and instead has a de-sexed physical persona, and she manages to subvert sexual stereotypes more successfully than other women rappers. While other women in music videos featuring Elliott are sexualized, she rarely is; another example of this phenomenon is the scene in "Work It" where Elliott raps "Girls girls, get that cash/Rather it's 9–5 or shaking that ass/ain't no shame/ ladies do your thang/just make sure you're ahead of the game" while two women are pole dancing at a strip club. Instead of pole dancing, Elliott is counting cash as she walks toward the camera, taking on the "madam" persona that she did in "Lady Marmalade." I will discuss this crucial scene later in the chapter.

Black women rappers have used the slave-owning trope to subvert these stereotypes; slave-ownership, specifically in the United States, is an act associated with white men and to a much, much lesser extent white women—black people, especially black women, are not thought of as participating in slave-ownership or characterizing themselves as owning slaves literally or metaphorically.[7] On the surface, it seems as if black women rappers are playing into stereotypes of black woman-ness, but a closer inspection of their lyrics proves how they simultaneously utilize the political and witty characteristics of hip hop music to challenge negative perceptions of black women's bodies. Nikki Lane analyzes how the black women body is "constructed as a site of spectacle and tension, even within the Black, hip hop community" and argues that black women rappers have to work within a gendered system that dehumanizes their bodies (782). She argues that rappers such as Trina and Lil' Kim are discussing complex subject matter in their music but need the allure of their bodies to attract people to their message. In other words, the jezebel stereotype that their image suggests is merely a cover. I would like to further Lane's analysis by interrogating how black women rappers use the slave-owning trope to draw attention to the plight of women rappers within the hip hop music genre in particular and the music industry as a whole.

Harriet Thugman: Rap Purist

Rah Digga (Rashia Fisher) is a women rapper from Newark, New Jersey, who rose to prominence at the turn of the millennium as a member of Flipmode Squad, a hip hop group led by Busta Rhymes. She released two albums: *Dirty Harriet* (2000) and *Classic* (2010). She was distinguished from women rappers such as Lil' Kim and Foxy Brown because her image did not revolve around her body and sexuality but rather highlighted aggressive lyrics and intellectual word play. Although Rah Digga did wear short skirts and low cut blouses in her music videos, the emphasis was on her captivating and abrasive lyrics, not her body, as opposed to most women rappers during this time. Digga dubs herself "Harriet Thugman," which interestingly places a celebrated slaver figure into a new millennium, hip hop context where many rapper's champion rebellion and originality. In an interview explaining why she chose this moniker, Rah Digga explains the need "to show I have an intellectual and positive side . . . I guess the use of profanities and my tone of voice may come across as hardcore. I wanted people to see that I'm actually positive and I'm not desecrating the memory of Harriet Tubman" (Hip Online Interview 2000). Digga's explanation conflates a hardcore voice and profanity usage with dumbness, as if she wants to separate herself from rappers who possess these same qualities but whose lyrics lack substance. The need for others to classify her as a conscious rapper is a theme that she raps about often, especially in "Harriet Thugman." Digga explicitly tackles issues of black inequality and how those issues are reminiscent of the brutality slaves faced. She affirms the idea that a black women rapper can dress provocatively and still have fans pay attention to the messages in her songs rather than her body, though one could argue that this is the reason why she did not gain mass mainstream appeal. She encompasses the idea of postmodern identity through her dueling identities; her image and lyrics blend hyper-masculinity with hyper-femininity and oppression with oppressor characteristics. Rah Digga is an underrated, highly skilled rapper that many scholars ignore when analyzing subversive women rappers. Hardcore hip hop heads love Digga and many consider *Dirty Harriet* a classic album, but she is not a heavily discussed rapper in academia.

My analysis of Digga will focus on her 2000 song "Harriet Thugman" which appears on the album *Dirty Harriet* (Elektra). Despite the explicit reference to the popular 1970s Clint Eastwood movie series, *Dirty Harriet*'s album cover instead contains imagery reminiscent of slavery: Digga is standing front and center of the cover with chains around her. Although the chains and hooks are technically the meat hooks used to secure large animal carcasses for butchering, they also look similar to the mechanics inside arcade claw machines. Digga is positioned as if she is a one of the items "up for grabs'—a literal piece of property—inside the claw machine. Her body language seems passive but simultaneously cunning—the hand on her face suggesting vulnerability, but she also stares directly in the eyes of viewers as though she is challenging them. The seemingly African style print and coloring of her dress, along with the braids and the leather jacket, makes Digga look like a kind of Millennial African Griot. On a symbolic level, the chains and meat hooks certainly communicate commodification—getting trapped within those chains leads to life as a slave, as property, an analogy that many rappers also draw upon in their lyrics. Yet, the image on the cover emphasizes that Digga has avoided capture by the menacing iron chains and hooks.

In doing so, it offers an iconic visual representation of the song "Harriet Thugman" (released without an accompanying video), and the subversive acts she raps about having to commit in order to organize a successful slave rebellion.

The singles from *Dirty Harriet* released with accompanying music videos were "Tight," "Imperial," and "Break Fool." Artists, in conjunction with record executives, usually choose songs that are upbeat and catchy as singles—this makes them more compatible for radio play and marketing purposes. Rap singles, in particular, gravitate toward being "club-bangers"— songs that are played in a club setting that people can dance and sing along to. I imagine that Rah Digga did not choose "Harriet Thugman" as a single because it is a short song (1:28) that doesn't contain a catchy chorus or refrain, which makes it the antithesis of Missy Elliott's "Work It," the other song I analyze in this chapter. "Harriet Thugman" features a sample from soul and funk singer Lou Courtney's 1967 song "I've Got Just the Thing," which gives it a soulful, laid back sound that makes the subversive slave rebellion she raps about seem calm and smooth.

Transforming Spaces of Oppressions into Places of Power

The subversion is introduced in the very first lines of "Harriet Thugman," in which Digga states:

> *I be that house nigga squatting in the lab/Rhymes comin, rhymes goin like I was a dollar cab/Fingerin the man tryin to tap into his spirit/A misguided soul so ain't checkin for the lyrics*

Digga takes the traditionally disempowered image of the women house slave, flips it, and turns it into position of empowerment. Suggesting that women rappers, like the original house slaves, use their position "inside the house/ power structure" to subvert these male dominated spaces. Digga's "house nigga" comparison, according to James Patterson, is "an analogy that requires some understanding of the kind of commitment that becoming a successful recording artist demands and the challenges of artist development for women within technological spaces often owned, operated, and managed by men" (70). And while like Patterson, I am interested in Digga's investment in challenging the status quo, Patterson's analysis emphasizes Digga's commitment to using physical underground spaces as empowerment, while my literary analysis project focuses on how Digga uses the imagery and language of slavery to discuss the transformation of oppressed spaces into sites of power—a common theme in many antebellum slave narratives.

Digga positions herself as a house slave, confounding the assumed clear distinctions between field slave and house slave. By calling herself a "house nigga" and placing herself inside the plantation, in close proximity to the male plantation owner, I'd argue that Digga is classifying herself as a plantation mistress but is challenging the white plantation mistress trope by showing how she uses rebellion to dismantle the slave system, while white plantation mistresses are often represented as reinforcing it. When discussing the role of white plantation mistresses, Clinton describes how southern planters "urged their women to do good works and promote benevolence," though "this effort was to extend no farther than the boundaries of the plantation" (11). Digga appropriates this trope by demonstrating that her benevolence challenges plantation boundaries—she will use her house slave status to help her fellow slaves escape. Although Clinton's analysis is useful, she does not discuss how the plantation mistress trope is complicated when it is occupied by a black woman. When discussing the resistance of black women slaves, Angela Davis notes their attempts to poison the food of their masters and set fire to the plantation. In order to poison and serve the food, the woman must be in close proximity to the house and slave master, which demonstrates how women slaves used their house slave/plantation mistress status as a method of subversion. In a hip hop context, Digga turns the plantation mistress trope into an intelligent, scheming black women house slave that evades capture while committing illegal acts.

She draws parallels between slaves' illegal acts, such as squatting, to contemporary dollar cabs, which are unregistered, illegal taxis. Although Digga is secretly writing "in the lab," her intellect is flowing steadily the way dollar cabs receive steady customers while avoiding arrest. "The man" refers to the owner of the plantation, and "ain't checkin' for the lyrics" demonstrates that the owner is oblivious of Digga's lyricism, which speaks to the subversive nature of communication styles among slaves. This is similar to how slaves read in secret because they are forbidden to publicly—Digga has to keep her intellect a secret if she wants her slave rebellion to succeed. "Squatting" is a gesture utilized by slaves in slave narratives, and in this context, I define squatting as a slave's need to stay hidden inside of someone else's property in order to commit illegal acts like reading and writing. In particular, Harriet Jacobs writes of her experience squatting in a secluded domestic area for seven years in *Incidents in the Life of a Slave Girl, Written by Herself*. Jacobs flees from Mr. Flint, her white male slave-owner, and she writes letters to him from a fake address in New York with the intention of thwarting his search efforts. The house Jacobs squats in is of close proximity to Mr. Flint, and even though Jacobs is mentally chained by slavery, like Digga is, both writers use subversive written communication to divert their owners' attention from their rebellion. Toward the end of Digga's song, the slave rebellion is successful, and Digga leads "a nation up north where the real party at" similarly to how Jacobs flees up north and escapes from her owner. They turn spaces of oppression into places of power and subversion.

Rah Digga and Linguistic Superiority

Digga continues to discuss her qualification:

> *Many different players, only one hold the ball/ Ghetto fabulous chick, go against the protocol/ With the grittiest lingo, still such a little sweetheart/ Book educated with a whole lotta street smarts*

In this verse, Digga champions her leadership skills, intellect, and independence. The most fascinating aspect of this verse is how she celebrates the fluidity and duality of her identity. She celebrates both community and individuality when she raps about sports players who, in order to win, must work together but still pull their weight individually, which was also the case during antebellum slavery. The leader, the one holding the ball, is Digga. As Ruth A. Banes argues, antebellum slave narrators had to appeal to multiple audiences (northern abolitionists and the slave community) but "the ability to imagine oneself within more than one role was a basis for the slave's self-worth, especially within the black community" (62). Like slave narrators, Digga presents an argument that she can juggle multiple roles: she can use her acting skills to trick her slave-master into trusting her and diverting his attention from her rebellion, she can use her sophisticated and swift vocabulary to convince slaves to follow her, and she can use her street smarts to find the path to freedom.

Digga continues her boosting by describing herself as "ghetto fabulous," a term frequently used term in hip hop music that challenges assumptions of ghetto life as trashy and undesirable. "Ghetto" is a pejorative term synonymous with trashy and tacky. It describes something of low value and worth. "Fabulous" refers to something that is extraordinary and desirable. The terms mixed together represent an attempt to transform the offensiveness of the word "ghetto" into a phrase of positive reclamation. Roopali Mukherjee describes the ghetto fabulous aesthetic as "a quintessential product of the post-soul era" that "survives as a meticulously groomed signifier of youth rebellion, evidence of rebelliousness itself transformed into a formulaic, and profitable, market commodity" (601). Through the term "ghetto fabulous," the lower class black experience becomes a product that is celebrated rather than devalued. The aesthetic was popularized by rap artists such as P. Diddy, Fabolous, and Mystikal; however, although many of these artists grew up poor, they were wealthy musicians at the time that they were pushing this aesthetic, making them willing participants in the commodification of hip hop in particular and the black experience as a whole.[8] By describing herself as a "ghetto fabulous chick" who goes "against the protocol," Digga enters this debate about ghetto fabulousness by asserting her independence; the aesthetic is trendy around the time Digga releases "Harriet Thugman," but she plans to package her aesthetic differently than other rappers. She emphasizes her leadership and rebellion against both the norms of the hip hop industry and antebellum slavery. Slave-owners do not want rebellious slaves just like leaders of the music industry do not want rebellious music artists. She uses this song to challenge preconceived notions about slaves' docility and women rappers' position in the hip hop industry. In interviews, Digga discusses her rapping style as a way of showing how women rappers should not have to rely on their sexuality to get their message across (Patterson 70).

Digga is essentially presenting an argument that she deserves to lead the slave rebellion and rap industry because of her ability to successfully navigate competing identities; even though Digga has "the grittiest lingo," she is still "such a sweetheart." Although Digga challenges the idea that women rappers lack substance and dress too provocatively, her aesthetic is feminine. Unlike women rappers such as Boss, Lady of Rage, and Da Brat (at the beginning of her career), she does not adopt a masculine appearance and instead wears skirts, dresses, makeup, and heels in her music videos. Katie Mullins argues that this is why Digga is a fascinating artist to discuss; her album *Dirty Harriet* "set a standard for women at the beginning of a decade that saw a decrease in both the lyrical talent and the number of women rap artists receiving commercial attention" (426). Digga proves that black women rappers can create lyrically aggressive and profound music while still keeping a feminine aesthetic. In both a new millennium context and slavery context, "book educated" black people are a threat to white hegemony. "Book educated" black people with "street smarts" are even more of a threat because they can navigate both the hegemonic education system and the code of the streets. Geneva Smitherman argues that black rappers' use of African American Vernacular is not an indicator of lack of education but is rather an attempt to "disturb the peace": "Because many rap artists are college educated, and most are adept at code switching, they obviously could employ 'standard English' in their rap lyrics. However, in their quest to 'disturb the peace,' they deliberately and consciously employ the 'anti-language' of the Black speech community, thus socio-linguistically constructing themselves as members of the dispossessed" (11). Smitherman's analysis defines Digga's educational background and rap style since Digga is studying to become an electrical engineer before her rap career blossoms. Digga linguistically blends traditional rap slang with European-American language in her lyrics, hence her usage of terms like "ghetto fabulous," grittiest lingo," and "book educated." She alludes to her ability to code switch, which makes her the perfect candidate to lead rebellions because she can hide her intellect from slave-masters while speaking the language of fellow slaves. The concept of code-switching arguably originated during antebellum slavery; Smitherman details the origins of African American language and its product as a blend of European American English and the Niger-Congo family of African languages: "The result of this blend was a communication system that functioned as both a resistance language and a linguistic bond of cultural and racial solidarity for those born under the lash" (8). This blending of languages is crucial to Digga; she recognizes the importance of being well versed in the language of the slaves and the slave-masters: a successful rebellion requires a linguistic navigation of both worlds.

Rah Digga's Transformation from Slave to Slave-Owner

After presenting her argument for why she is a capable and intelligent leader, Digga becomes a trailblazer, like Harriet Tubman, and raps,

> *Follow me now, as I build my fanbases/ Makin rappers worry like they got open cases/Harriet Thugman, bout to see shit through/ Like a whole world of people wait for Episode 2*

This is where slave-ownership language subtly creeps into "Harriet Thugman." Digga is assembling followers who will listen to her message and accompany her up north. The next line focuses on how Digga wants to dismantle her competition by instilling fear into them. "Open cases" refer to court activity that the rappers are involved in. The rappers are paranoid that these open cases will lead to jail time. Of course, slave rebellions and the acts associated with plotting a rebellion (reading, organizing, and writing) were illegal. This line suggests that the rappers Digga refer to may have been inadequate leaders because they were caught by the system, hence why they have open cases. Digga is reiterating her ability to lead a successful rebellion by capitalizing on the failures of her predecessors. She also emphasizes her resilience and encourages the listener to follow her. The listeners are part of the "whole world of people" who are waiting to see if her rebellion succeeds.

Now that Digga has a significant following, she is more selective about who is allowed to join her rebellion:

> *I be the rap purist, the walking hip hop thesaurus/The innovator, spawned from Libra and Taurus/Do away cats with the same ol' wack/Lead a nation up north where the real party at*

This verse serves two purposes: to highlight Digga's ability to juggle dual identities as well as create criteria for her followers' actions and character- istics. She is a "walking hip hop thesaurus": thesauruses contain synonyms and antonyms and Digga emphasizes her ability to participate in linguistic mobility—she can navigate physical and linguistic challenges as she and her followers journey up north. Written communication becomes embodied here as a form of personification, an ontological metaphor that "allows us to comprehend a wide variety of experiences with nonhuman entities in terms of human motivations, characteristics, and activities" (Lakoff 33). Digga takes on the language of slave-owning once her slave rebellion is successful, brag- ging that she will "Do away cats with the same ol' wack." Plantation owners had specific criteria for what type of slaves they wanted to buy, and now that Digga is the leader of the slave rebellion, she is allowed to make similar decisions—people who are "wack" are not allowed to come up north with her "where the real party at." Digga raps that she is a "rap purist" and "innova- tor," and those who do not possess these qualities do not fit her criteria for coming up north with her. Digga's conception of "rap purity" mirrors the concept of racial purity during American slavery; Catherine Clinton observes how "In a biracial slave society . . . 'racial purity' was a defining characteris- tic of the master class" (6). Although black women were raped by white male slave-owners and forced to bare children, they were not considered part of the master class and neither were their children since children's slave status was determined by their mother's positioning. In other words, the members of the master class wanted to remain white and untainted by African blood. Digga wants to bring people who are rap purists and innovators like herself up north, creating a new pure master class, similar to what the master class wanted during slavery. When placed in a slavery context where the concept of "purity" is laced with racial, hierarchical language, Rah Digga's description of herself as a "rap purist" complicates her liberator image.

"HARRIET THUGMAN" AS A POSTMODERN CONSTRUCTION OF A SLAVE/SLAVE-OWNER

"Harriet Thugman" highlights postmodern conceptions of identity and space. Postmodern theories of identity and space focus on how these entities are destabilized and therefore difficult to classify. In his analysis of postmodern identity in *The Simpsons*, Brian L. Ott explains how postmodern identity is not merely a rejection of modernism but rather consists of "a range of spaces between the outward projection of a relatively stable and essential self, grounded in inherited and pre-given categories, and the performance of a flexible and radically under-determined self, located in images and styles"

(62). Applying this definition of postmodern identity to "Harriet Thugman," Digga adapts a persona of a slave rebellion leader—tough, resilient, compassionate, and intelligent but simultaneously demonstrates the flexibility of her image by characterizing herself as elitist and unwelcoming of those who do not fit into her conception of rap purity. The duality of her identity highlights Digga's adherence to pre-constructed categories as well as her ability to destabilize them simultaneously, hence why she uses both conventions of slave-owning and being a slave. "Harriet Thugman" proves Digga's fluid identity and her ability to occupy competing identities. She is oppressed by the music industry and slavery because of her gender and skin tone. She oppresses others who do not have her level of vocabulary or who do not fit into her image of rap purity. The criteria that Digga creates for determining who can join her slave rebellion mirrors the process slave-owners use to inspect slaves to determine their worth. She is a slave to inequality but a metaphorical slave-owner to less skilled rappers. She challenges preconceived notions of constructions of slave-ownership and the plantation mistress trope.

THE ALLURE OF MISSY ELLIOTT

Missy "Misdemeanor" Elliott is a rapper, song-writer, actress, producer, and director who hails from Portsmouth, Virginia. She is popular in the late '90s and early '00s for her multiple music industry talents as well as her catchy song lyrics and outrageous music videos. From music fans who enjoy her women empowerment aesthetic to academic scholars who are fascinated by her lyrical skills, Elliott's vast appeal makes her the ideal artist to analyze for this study opposite of Rah Digga. Contrary to Rah Digga, Elliott has enjoyed a massive amount of mainstream success not only in the music industry but in the fashion, social media, and business worlds as well. Although both were affiliated with the same record label (Elektra) during this time, Elliott's image was more fun and playful than Rah Digga's, which might explain why Elliott was able to cross-over to pop music more easily than Rah Digga. Elliott also wrote and produced songs with several mainstream artists such as Janet Jackson, Aaliyah, Jay-Z, and Ciara.

Elliott's "Work It," was published in 2002, two years after *Dirty Harriet*, so it's not a stretch to assume that she may have been influenced by Rah Digga to engage with slavery themes in her song. Unlike "Harriet Thugman," "Work It" has an accompanying music video and was an enormous mainstream hit—Elliott won several awards, including Video of the Year and Best Hip Hop Video at the 2003 MTV Music Video Awards and a Grammy Award for Best Women Rap Solo Performance in 2004.[9] "Work It" also contains a catchy chorus as well as an eclectic blend of '80s hip hop and millennial club banging beats—the song samples Run D.M.C.'s "Peter Piper" and Rock Master Scott & the Dynamic Three's "Request Line." The song popularized many phrases, including "badonkadonk," "I put my thing down, flip it and reverse it," and "get your hair did." I will examine Elliott's wordplay and linguistic choices later on in the chapter.

Elliott and Digga were frequent collaborators—they appeared on the tracks "Touch It (Remix)," "Party & Bullshit (Remix)," and "Pussycat" together. In July 2016, VH1 Hip Hop Honors featured tributes to Missy Elliott as well as Queen Latifah, Lil' Kim, and Salt n Pepa, and Digga was one of the performers who paid homage to them. Because of their professional and personal connections, I chose Digga and Elliott as the stars of this chapter. I am interested in why Elliott was a more mainstream compatible artist than Digga. Digga's slavery references are more overt and challenging than Elliott's, and I propose that is the reason why she wasn't as popular. Digga's usage of the slave-owing trope is also more subversive than Elliott—although Elliott usage is interesting and at times subversive, there are also ways in which she represents stereotypical notions of black womanhood, specifically black womanhood in hip hop culture.

Elliott as Madam and Omniscient Narrator

As I briefly mentioned earlier, during the late '90s and early 2000s, Elliott[10] was also a co-star on several hip hop and R&B songs where she played the omniscient narrator whose confidential information gave her power over the other subjects in the songs. Elliott raps on the chorus of Memphis Bleek's 2000 song "Is That Your Chick?"[11] where the premise revolves around a man's girlfriend cheating on him with the other male rappers on the song (Memphis Bleek, Jay-Z, and Twista on the album version). Elliott describes the various provocative, sexual acts that the woman commits with these men and asks the man "Is that your chick?" taunting him with information that he is not privy to. In the music video for the song, Elliott is attending a party and spends most of her time sitting on the couch, observing others. Toward the end of the song, she looks directly into the camera and makes the viewers follow her to the window of the apartment where the "chick" she is referring to is outside of the apartment window begging to get into the party. This solidifies Elliott's role as omniscient narrator by demonstrating how she knows everything that is going on at the party, even information about the woman's cheating that the partner doesn't know about. The viewer is synonymous with the oblivious partner as if we are also supposed to be outraged by the woman's licentious actions while simultaneously basking in Elliott's all-knowing persona.

In a song that I consider less offensive and more empowering, Elliott is featured in the music video for singer Tweet's 2002 song "Oops (Oh My)," a controversial song about women self-love and masturbation[12] that Elliott co-wrote with her. Elliott raps a call and response third verse with Tweet: "I looked over to my left (sung by Tweet)/Mmm, I was lookin' so good I couldn't reject myself (rapped by Elliott)/I looked over to my left (sung by Tweet)/Mmm, I was feelin' so good I had to touch myself (rapped by Elliott)." Tweet is alone while singing her part, and when she looks over to the left, she sees Elliott inside of a mirror rapping her verse. Elliott acts as a metaphor for a mirror, an object that sees things no one else can or distorts images (the concept of a crazy mirror or fun house mirror). Masturbation is typically conceptualized as an act committed solo, so Elliott, as the omniscient narrator again, is privy to information that most people will not see, especially since women masturbation is still a taboo topic in the United States. She's encouraging Tweet's act of self-love.

While both "Is That Your Chick?" and "Oops (Oh My)" suggest that Elliott has ownership over other characters in the video and a puppet master, they do not contain the overt references to slavery and slave-ownership that "Work It," which appears on her 2002 album *Under Construction*, does. My analysis of "Work It" will discuss both the slavery imagery present in the music video as well as the lyrics that appear on the album version of the song since the music video and album version contain slightly different lyrics. The slave-owning trope adds an interesting angle to Elliott's omniscient narrator role that helps explain her complicated relationship with the music industry. Several rappers have drawn parallels to how the industry enslaves them but not as many discuss how the privileges they receive from the industry helps them wield power metaphoric to slave-ownership over others[13].

Elliott's Reconceptualization of the Plantation Mistress Trope

In the first verse of "Work It," Elliott is courting a man she is interested in, which reverses antebellum white dating conventions by making the woman the aggressor and the man a passive recipient of her advances. Elliott raps:

> *I'd like to get to know ya so I could show ya/ Put the pussy on ya like I told ya/ Give me all your numbers so I can phone ya/ Your girl acting stank, then call me ova*

Elliott sets herself up as a mistress. The man she's courting is in a relationship with another woman, but this does not stop Elliott from wanting to sexually pursue him. Elliott asks for "all" of the man's numbers so she can phone him, suggesting that he is dating women besides Elliott and living multiple secret lives. This also relates to Elliott's omniscient narrator persona—she wants "all" of his numbers so she can keep tabs on him. She needs to know what he is doing at all times.

Later on in the song, Elliott continues her courtship by suggesting that she and the man get drunk together:

> *Boy, lift it up, let's make a toast-a/Let's get drunk, that's gonna bring us closer/*
> *Don't I look like a Halle Berry poster/See the Belvedere playing tricks on you*

Right before "Work It" was released, Elliott lost a significant amount of weight and told interviewers that one motivation she had for losing weight was so she could dance in her music videos. Elliott is more active in this video than in previous ones. Around this time, *Monster's Ball* featuring Halle Berry was released with some critics arguing that the only reason why Berry received Oscar nominations for this role was because of her character's disturbing and wild sex scene with Billy Bob Thornton. Berry was also accused of changing her image to appeal to a whiter, mainstream audience. This could also be a metaphor for how the music industry shapes artists' images to the point of unrecognition. Similar to how alcohol impairs judgment, industry influences can make Elliott shape-shift into another person; alcohol brings the man closer to an artificial version of Elliott rather than a genuine image.

As I mentioned earlier, Elliott often plays an omniscient narrator/madam role in music videos, and this role is a heavy factor in "Work It":

> *Girls, girls, get that cash/If it's 9 to 5 or shaking your ass/Ain't no shame, ladies*
> *do your thing/Just make sure you ahead of the game*

As Elliott raps this line, she stands between two pole-dancing women. Elliott walks up to the camera and starts counting her cash. However, Elliott is not pole-dancing, nor is she wearing revealing clothing—instead, she is wearing Adidas brand clothing, popularized by Run D.M.C., LL Cool J, and other '80s rap artists. This represents her dueling identity—she brands herself with mainstream clothing while chastising the music industry for not letting her personalize her image; thus, her image becomes intertwined with Adidas. Slave-owners are classified as branding others, not being branded themselves, and this demonstrates how the slave-owner/plantation mistress trope is complicated when placed in a twenty-first-century hip hop context—Elliott is a slave to mainstream branding while simultaneously showing how she enslaves others, demonstrated by her characterization as a madam.

Earlier in "Work It," Elliott makes a distinction between herself and other people who sell their bodies for cash when she explains how she's "not a prostitute" but can "give you what you want." Elliott is not positioned as an equal with the pole-dancing women, and she counts the cash as if she is a madam that benefits from other women's objectification. Although Elliott supports sex workers, strippers, and other provocative professions involving sexuality by telling women to have no shame, she does not want to be mistaken for a sex worker.

The financial benefits Elliott receives as a madam is reminiscent of the privileges plantation mistresses receive during antebellum slavery. Although plantation mistresses are oppressed by a gendered hierarchal slaver system that places women below men, there are financial advantages to partaking in this system, including the acquisition of property. Clinton recognizes how in the master class, "sons received land and daughters, slaves" and thus, white women are slave-owners who can inherit property from their families (37). When referencing Harriet Beecher Stowe's *Uncle Tom's Cabin*, Sandra Gilbert and Susan Gubar in *Madwoman in the Attic: The Woman Writer and the Nineteenth-Century Literary Imagination* say that Uncle Tom's " . . . secret prayers and suicidal passivity constitute, moreover, a distinctively feminine response to coercion, a response illuminated by Stowe's critique of slavery as a patriarchal institution in which both slaves and wives - and slaves who function as wives and wives who function like slaves - are used and abused" (483). Stowe's critique of slavery focuses on the oppression that both slave and free women face and highlights how difficult it was for women to become slave-owners if they were not married or did not come from a family with a strong line of white male slave-owners.

Slave-Owning Language Adds a New Dimension to Elliott's Madam Persona

Referring back to the hook of the song, Elliott answers the question of "Is it worth it?" later in this verse:

> *Just cause I got a lot of fame super/Prince couldn't get me change my name papa/Kunta Kinte a slave again, no sir/Picture black's saying, Oh yes'a massa (No!)*

She firmly roots her place in the music industry by saying she's still "Supa Dupa Fly" (the name of her first album released in 1997). She answers by saying that yes, it's worth it to continue making mainstream music because Elliott has the power to work within these strict guidelines by using creative wordplay in her music. In his review of *Under Construction*, John Bush praises Elliott for turning "the tables on male rappers, taking charge of the sex game, matching their lewdest, rudest rhymes, and also featuring the most notorious backmasked vocal of the year" (*AllMusic*—Review). Many people were fascinated by Elliott's vocal talent in "Work It," so much that in his 2002 song "The Rap Up," rapper Skillz suggests that there was "War time, Bush wanting actions/ But we was too busy worried about what Missy was saying backwards" (Skillz—"The Rap Up" Lyrics). In other words, Elliott was a huge focal point during this year and she took precedent over more pressing issues such as the war in Iraq. Elliott's backwards lyrics demonstrate her ability to use words subversively. This is similar to how slaves used communication styles unknown by their owners in order to rebel against the establishment. Unlike Prince,[14] Elliott blends her current *Under Construction* persona with her *Supa Dupa Fly* one, alluding to the idea that identity is fluid and both of these personas are part of her music image. The title *Under Construction* also suggests that Elliott's image hasn't finished developing, and we should anticipate a revitalized sound in the future.

The previous section demonstrates Elliott's construction as a madam while this section blends her madam persona with slave-ownership language and imagery. "Massa" initially refers to a white male slave master. However, "massa" is also referring to the music industry. The most famous scene of *Roots* shows Kunta Kinte being beaten until he accepts his new Anglicized name, Tobey. This draws a striking parallel between the economic conditions of slaves and mainstream hip hop artists. Changing one's image to sell more records or appease white executives is akin to slavery where slaves had no control over their identity. However, the color-shifting that occurs in the music video of "Work It" makes us question the identity of "massa"—we assume "massa" is white since slave-owners in American culture are commonly represented as white, but he ends up being a self-hating black man.

The shapeshifting from white male slave-owner to black male slave-owner conjures up images of racial mimicry. In *Black Skins, White Masks*, Frantz Fanon describes the relationship between black men and white men as "dual narcissism," suggesting that black men and white men rely on each other for social gains: "White men consider themselves superior to black men. . . . Black men want to prove to white men, at all costs, the richness of their thought, the equal value of their intellect" (3). In other words, white men need a scapegoat to feel superior to while black men need a leader to worship and mimic. I read this scene in "Work It" as a reminder that some black people are content with being oppressors and adapting hegemonic white supremacist values. There are black artists who are willing to do the work of disempowering black people for the benefit of white people. These people are known as "self-haters."

Elliott's Objectification and Exploitation of Women

After Elliott lyrically dismantles the music industry, she solidifies her position as Queen of Hip Hop:

> *Admit I'm the F_____ name won the battle/When I drop this record here, you won't even matter*[15]

The music video to "Work It" was released two months before *Under Construction* dropped, but Elliott gave everyone a taste of dual identities. She's mixing *Supa Dupa Fly* with *Under Construction*, her weight loss did not make her a slave to the music industry, and her skills are so good that her success will eclipse other rappers.

Elliott participates in the objectification and commodification of women by using language reminiscent of slavery to position herself as a madam who exploits women. Similar to Digga, she boasts about being lyrically superior to fellow slaves (rappers) and provides concrete reasons why she is a dominant force in hip hop music. She positions herself as a madam "Work It" and "Harriet Thugman" are post-neo-slave narratives told from the perspective of women rappers forging an identity that aligns their oppression with their oppressive techniques. Both songs outline a journey from bondage to freedom, but freedom now entails the ability to metaphorically enslave others. The narratives' construction of postmodern identity and discussion of millennial inequalities is what makes these songs post-neo-slave narratives rather than neo-slave narratives. Rather than adhere to strict categories of identity, Digga and Elliott show the fluidity of these categories: black women can fight against slavery and the music industry while simultaneously discriminating against those who do not fit into their conception of rap purity.

"Don't I Look Like a Halle Berry Poster?"

The hip hop-neo-slave narrative vs. the post-neo-slave narrative

L.H. Stallings proposes the concept of a "hip-hop neo-slave narrative" and defines it as combining "the fugitive slave's narrative with the free ex-slaves narrative, as well as linking the autobiographical with the fictionalized. It accomplishes the neo-slave narratives assessment of economic slavery, in addition to the original slaver narratives discussion of chattel slavery" (187).[16] She also takes issue with how scholars "forgo an analysis of the genre's authors as neo-slaves" and argues that black artists are drawing attention to the neo-slave conditions they face such as mass incarceration, the war on drugs, and housing discrimination (188). While Stallings mostly applies her argument to Donald Goines, the author of 1972's *Whoreson: The Story of a*

Ghetto Pimp and his real life imprisonment, I am interested in how this definition is challenged when placed in conversation with post-neo-slave narratives. Elliott and Digga, for example, channel the fugitive slave and the free
ex-slave in their lyrics, but they simultaneously conjure up the slave-owner
narrative as well, which demonstrates their willingness to engage with both
their subjugation and power.

Stallings's definition also focuses on how the characters in hip hop
neo-slave narratives experience bondage but not necessarily how they participate in bonding others. Though many rappers come from impoverished backgrounds, they are still selling an image and product to their fans that is not
indicative of their actual lived experiences. They are indeed oppressed by a
hegemonic music industry that mirrors antebellum slavery but are also aiding
in the oppression of others. As I outlined in the introduction, I am referring
to these texts as post-neo-slave narratives because this term more accurately
encompasses how characters' identity is based on fluidity rather than fixed
notions of categorization as well as how original definitions of neo-slave
narratives did not account for millennial non-literary texts such as film and
music. Stallings accurately suggests that the reason why hip hop fiction and
songs have not made it into the black academic literary canon is because of
class elitism, which is why she proposes the "hip-hop-neo-slave narrative"
concept. I am aware of hip hop's history as a truth-telling and truth-seeking
genre of music where many rappers discuss real issues they've encountered
but we must also acknowledge the excessive amount of exaggeration and
falsehood that occurs in the genre as well. I have enhanced Stallings's definition by examining postmodern notions of identity construction and their relationship to the post-neo-slave narrative.

Digga and Elliott's Post-Neo-Slave Narratives

To reiterate, I define post-neo-slave narratives as texts that blend the
neo-slave narrative with postmodern notions of identity and performativity
and are distinguished from other neo-slave narratives in that these texts apply
millennial theories of identity to the portrayal of slaves while embracing connections with visual texts, unlike the original concept of a neo-slave narrative.
Neo-slave narratives focused on the oppression slaves faced rather than the
methods they used to oppress others.

"Harriet Thugman" is a post-neo-slave narrative due to its meshing of
identity categories and the narrator's journey from bondage to freedom to an
elitist that evokes slave-owning language. Digga uses this language when she
provides strict criteria for who can and cannot join her journey toward freedom. The postmodern identity from slave to slave-owner that she constructs

allows her to successfully plot and execute her slave rebellion and establish herself as a leader in hip hop and, like Harriet Tubman, in antebellum slavery. "Work It" contains a sharp critique of the music industry that characterizes it as an institution of slavery. Elliott uses the slave-owning trope to brag about lyrically enslaving her haters while simultaneously describing the methods the music industry uses to keep her down. She performs a madam/omniscient narrator persona that is reminiscent of how slave-owners exploited their slaves for financial gain while trying to prove how slaves were inferior.

For Elliott and Digga, it is their ability to think and act like slaves that increases their aptitude for slave-ownership, which emphasizes how postmodern identity restructures the conception of slave-owners. This is a new way of re-conceptualizing power and representations of ownership, as both rappers challenge conventions of postmodern identity while answering Patricia Hill Collins's call for the creation of postmodern language that critique notions of power as well as provides a framework for empowering black women.

NOTES

1. Examples of this include Nicki Minaj's "I Feel Free," Da Brat's "I Was the One," and Gangsta Boo's "Can I Get Paid? (Stripper's Anthem)."

2. Scarlett O'Hara, the white plantation mistress in *Gone with the Wind*, is the most famous example of this characterization.

3. Although Lil' Kim was rapping in 1994, she did not gain mainstream appeal until the late '90s/early '00s.

4. Lil' Kim, though not the focus of this chapter, is an interesting case study for the question of if and how black women rappers can subvert stereotypes of black women in their music. She appears on Christina Aguilera's "Can't Hold Us Down" where her verse explicitly challenges the general public perception that women who sleep with multiple partners are hoes while promiscuous men are applauded. Simultaneously, she frequently chastises women who are promiscuous and calls women she beefs with bitches. In Mobb Deep's "Quiet Storm (Remix)," Kim boasts about her lyrical abilities while talking crap about "bitches [who] suck cock just to get to the top" (Mobb Deep—Lyrics). Lil' Kim and Nicki Minaj are currently involved in a well-publicized beef with each other as Kim feels that Minaj stole her image and is now capitalizing off of it, destroying the concept of women unity and solidifying the idea that there's only room for one hyper-sexed black women rapper at a time.

5. As Harris-Perry explains later on in the book, Ronald Reagan built much of his political platform on the Welfare Queen stereotype; essentially, he told Americans that he would control black women's bodies and take away their reproductive power if he was elected to office. Since the general American public still perceives black women as sexually devious and living off of the welfare system, Reagan was able to successfully capitalize on this stereotype.

6. In 1965, Daniel Patrick Moynihan issued *The Negro Family: The Case for National Action*, also known as "The Moynihan Report," a report commissioned by then President Lyndon Banes Johnson. The purpose of "The Moynihan Report" was to understand the connection between poverty and the black family structure. In the report, Moynihan concluded that the black community is in poverty because poor black people deviate from the traditional American family structure of the bread-winning father and stay-at-home mother. Dorothy Roberts argues that Moynihan "endowed poor Black women—the most subordinated members of society—with the power of a matriarch" and blamed poverty in the black community on black women (16). As a result, black women were characterized as deviant, and their private decisions were subject to public scrutiny, reinforcing the idea that black women are denied privacy and considered public property.

7. Hence the surprise when I tell people what my dissertation topic is about.

8. For more about the term "ghetto fabulous," see scholarship by Christopher Holmes Smith and Dick Hebdige.

9. The Grammy's recognition of hip hop as a credible genre of music is a fairly recent phenomenon. The Grammys began in 1959, though most scholars agree that hip hop wasn't formulated until the '70s. The first rap category for "Best Rap Performance" was in 1989, nearly two decades after its original conception. Critics have chastised the Grammys for ignoring black artists, specifically black rap artists. "Best Women Rap Solo Performance" was a Grammy category for only two years, which suggests that mainstream music is still unreceptive of women rap artists. Elliott won the award in 2003 and 2004 for the two years it was in place.

10. As I am close-reading Elliott's lyrics, I want to emphasize that I am referring to Elliott the music artist, not Elliott personally. This is an important distinction to make because it factors into my argument later on in the chapter about mediated authorship and identity in hip hop music. Some scholars make the mistake of assuming that every song a rapper makes is about her personal experience and ignores the imagined identities and stories that rappers often include in their work.

11. The purpose of this chapter is not to debate Elliott's feminist credibility, as I think debates about what is/isn't feminist are reductive and unfruitful. However, it's worth mentioning that although critics praise Elliott for her feminist and empowering songs, we cannot ignore her presence in offensive and misogynist music videos like this one. She supports many scholars' stance that mainstream hip hop is a deeply misogynist music genre that is extremely difficult for women rappers to subvert regardless of their genuine efforts to.

12. In interviews, Tweet denies that this song is about women masturbation, but no one buys her argument, especially with lyrics like "I was feeling so good I had to touch myself." I will utilize Roland Barthes's *Death of the Author* theory by de-centering the author and disagreeing with Tweet's assessment as the lyrics contradict her rationale.

13. This chapter focuses on black women rappers since the entire purpose of this research is to interrogate representations of women slave ownership in contemporary American popular culture. As a result, I did not conduct a rigorous search of male

rappers' usage of the slave-owning trope. This is an area of research I am interested in pursuing in the future.

14. R.I.P.

15. The music video and the album version contain different lines, but my reading focuses on the line featured in the music video because it emphasizes Elliott's fixation on the material aspects of lyrical ownership.

16. Hip hop artists often perform a persona that does not mirror their actual experiences. Authorship is mediated; both slave narrative authors and rappers had outside sources who heavily influenced their texts. Fictional accounts and lived experiences, while intertwined, are not always easy to discern. An interesting example of this is Elliott's "Gossip Folks" where she discusses rumors she's heard about herself but doesn't necessarily debunk those rumors, specifically the rumors about her sexuality. Stallings does acknowledge that editors, publishers, and marketers influence how texts are branded and marketed toward audiences, and these forms of branding are what Digga and Elliott are rebelling against.

Conclusion

TOWARD A BLACK FEMINIST COUNTERNARRATIVE

Kara Walker's work "Emancipation Approximation" (2000) series featured silhouettes that depict scenes from antebellum slavery. Walker cares less about mimicking slavery exactly as it was and more about taking creative liberties with her depiction of slavery. Because of this, it is possible for her to visualize a woman with an afro as the "top" of the plantation hierarchy. This aligns her with other artists in this book project, such as *12 Years a Slave* and *Rah Digga* who imagine slavery in a postmodern, twenty-first-century context. Postmodern identity theories provide a more nuanced look into Walker's work because we can see visualizations of black women in slight positions of agency, which complicates common readings of her work. In her analysis of Walker's work, Rachel Adams purports that "In her series 'Emancipation Approximation' (2000), a black female silhouette bends under the weight of a white figure wearing an enormous gown. This image literalizes the burden of a system that makes some women responsible for cleaning, grooming, and maintaining the health of others. Walker suggests that neither party is well served by this arrangement: the white woman is rendered immobile by her massive dress, while the black woman bends under the weight of her load." While I agree with Adams's interpretation that the silhouette demonstrates how the plantation slave system harms women of all races, the silhouette asks us to question the racial identity of each silhouette. This reading assumes that the silhouettes are inherently black or inherently white and does not consider the ways that Walker may push against race and gender categories. The hairstyle of the white silhouette looks like an afro puff. Perhaps the woman being thrown is more ambiguous and the women are not so black and white.

In this project, I argued for the creation of new language and criteria for analyzing twenty-first-century representations of slavery. A crucial element of post-neo-slave narratives is the emphasis on placing literary and visual texts in conversation with each other. Due to the interconnectedness of different genres in twenty-first-century culture, as demonstrated by how often the literary texts in this project reference visual culture and vice versa, it is imperative that a new genre of slavery representations is created to account for this complexity. The post-neo-slave narrative fills this crucial space by demonstrating the intertextual nature of literature and visual culture in slavery representations. Creating the post-neo-slave narrative subgenre provides the literary studies field with an alternative lens for critiquing and analyzing non-literary texts that did not fit the original definition of neo-slave narratives

Viewing female slave ownership through a postmodern framework allows the literary studies field to analyze the multifaceted nature of identity as women slave owners are oppressors and oppressed simultaneously. This also challenges the common American narrative that focuses on men's experiences as slaves and slave-owners by expanding on women's roles in representations of slave culture. The post-neo-slave narrative allows for more nuanced portrayals of black women, as "the early twenty-first century . . . is a time when, arguably, there is more space for African American writers to address the lesser-known and more sensitive issues of slavery that complicate the totalizing assumptions of black innocence and white complicity in its evil" (Crawford 76). Postmodern conceptions of identity as fluid and pluralistic make it possible for artists to portray black women as slave-owners, as this is now an identity category that is available to them.

The visual and multimedia texts that I analyze in this project only contain a small sample size of possibilities for the conception of post-neo-slave narratives. Scholars should extend my definition and analysis of post-neo-slave narratives to include other genres such as archives, online forums, video/board games, and coding/programming. This will aid in the creation of the post-neo-slave narrative genre—what texts should we include in this new subgenre?

I also encourage scholars to, unapologetically, engage in "mesearch." On a basic level, the concept of black women as slave-owners interests me because it feels as if most narratives about black women involve struggle, discrimination, and victimization. Black women owning slaves challenges this idea of black women as perpetual victims, as they become both oppressed and oppressor. I do not, by any means, want to diminish the real problems and issues that black women face, but the scholarly conversation surrounding black women should extend beyond how we function in this world as victims. This is also why I appreciate scholars like Joan Morgan who treat black women as complex people with agency. Morgan's article, "Why We Get Off: Moving Towards a Black Feminist Politics of Pleasure," argues that black feminist scholarship from the 1960s-2000s, while revolutionary and insightful, treats black women's bodies as a site of trauma, and black women engaging in pleasure is inherently traumatic. Although this book does not focus on black women and pleasure specifically, I am interested in examining narratives of black women that challenge, and ultimately overthrow, our victimization. A question I always ask myself is, "Why are multiple subject positions available to other groups but not black women?" I do not subscribe to this idea of colorblindness, at least not its twenty-first-century political usage, or that racism and sexism do not exist, but I also do not think black women should define our experiences by the discrimination we face. It gives our power away to external forces. Not every black woman fought against slavery or was part of the revolution. Some were Mistress Shaw. Doralise Derbanne. Caldonia. Their stories deserve a seat at the table as well.

Bibliography

Abrudan, Elena. "Postmodern Identity. Image, Fashion and New Technologies." *Journal of Media Research*, vol. 5, no.1, 2012, pp. 3–14.

Adams, Terry M. and Douglas B. Fuller. "The Words Have Changed but the Ideology Remains the Same: Misogynistic Lyrics in Rap Music." *Journal of Black Studies*, vol. 36, no.1, 2006, p.p. 938–957.

Alexander, Michelle. *The New Jim Crow: Mass Incarceration in the Age of Colorblindness*. New Press, 2010.

Als, Hilton. "The New Negro." *The New Yorker*, October 1997.

Antolini, Katherine Lane. "Scarlett O'Hara as Confederate Woman: The Evolution of War and Its Representation in Literature and Film." *West Virginia University Philological Papers*, vol. 51, no. 1, 2004, pp. 23–36.

Atkins, Leah Rawls. "High Cotton: The Antebellum Alabama Plantation Mistress and the Cotton Culture." *Agricultural History*, vol. 68, no. 2, 1994, pp 92–104.

Banes, Ruth A. "Antebellum Slave Narratives as Social History: Self and Community in the Struggle Against Slavery." *Journal of American Culture*, vol. 5, no. 2, 1982, pp. 62–70.

Banks, Ingrid. "Black Feminist Thought and Difference in the Third Wave: The Identity Politics of Postmodern Feminism and Colorblind Ideology." *Black Renaissance*, vol. 6, no. 1, 2004, p.p. 32–44.

Baraka, Amiri. *The Slave*, in *The Dutchman and the Slave*. HarperCollins, 1964.

Barnes, Paula C. "The Trope of the Mulatta Woman in the Cottage in Nineteenth-Century African American Literature." *Forum on Public Policy: A Journal of the Oxford Round Table*, 2010.

Baudrillard, Jean. *Simulations*. Translated by Paul Foss, Paul Patton, and Philip Beitchman. Semiotext(e), 1983.

Bauer, Margaret Donovan. *A Study of Scarletts: Scarlett O'Hara and Her Literary Daughters*. U of South Carolina P, 2014.

Bell, Bernard. *The Afro-American Novel and Its Traditions*. U of Massachusetts Press, 1989.

Bennett, Britt. "Ripping the Veil." *New Republic*, 2 Aug. 2016, newrepublic.com /article/135708/colson-whiteheads-fantastic-voyage. Accessed 3 Sep. 2016.

Bleek, Memphis. "Is That Your Chick (The Lost Verses) feat. Jay-Z, Missy Elliott, Twista" Lyrics." *AZ Lyrics* www.azlyrics.com/lyrics/memphisbleek/isthatyourchickthelostverses.html.

Bodden, Marlen Suyapa. *The Wedding Gift*. St. Martin's Griffin, 2013.

Bonyadi, Alireza. "Genre Analysis of Media Texts." *Procedia: Social and Behavioral Sciences*, vol. 66, no. 7, 2012, pp. 86–96.

Browne, Patrick T. J. ""To Defend Mr. Garrison": William Cooper Nell and the Personal Politics of Antislavery." *The New England Quarterly*, vol. 70, no. 3, 1997, p.p. 415–442.

Bush, John. "*Under Construction*-Missy Elliott Review." *All Music*, 4 Feb 2003, www.allmusic.com/album/under-construction-mw0000231192 Accessed 5 Oct 2014.

Butler, Judith. *Gender Trouble: Feminism and the Subversion of Identity*. Routledge, 1999.

Butler, Octavia. *Wild Seed*. Popular Library, 1980.

"*Cane River*—Lalita Tademy—Oprah's Book Club." *Oprah.com*, 20 Jun 2001, www.oprah.com/oprahsbookclub/cane-river-by-lalita-tademy.

Carby, Hazel V. *Reconstructing Womanhood: The Emergence of the Afro-American Woman Novelist*. Oxford UP, 1987.

ChallengingMedia. "bell hooks: Cultural Criticism and Transformation." Filmed [October 2006]. YouTube video, 6:02. Posted October 2006 www.youtube.com/watch?v=zQUuHFKP-9s.

Christian, Barbara. *New Black Feminist Criticism (1985–2000)*. Champaign: U of Illinois Press, 2000.

Clinton, Catherine. *The Plantation Mistress: Woman's World in the Old South*. Pantheon, 1982.

Colbert, Soyica Diggs, Robert J. Patterson, and Aida Levy Hussen, editors. *The Psychic Hold of Slavery: Legacies in American Expressive Culture*. Rutgers UP, 2016.

Collins, Patricia Hill. *Black Feminist Thought: Knowledge, Consciousness, and the Politics of Empowerment*. Boston: Unwin Hyman, 1990.

Collins, Patricia Hill. *Fighting Words: Black Women and the Search for Justice*. Minneapolis: U of Minnesota; 1998.

Crenshaw, Kimberlé. "Mapping the Margins: Intersectionality, Identity Politics, and Violence against Women of Color." *Stanford Law Review* 43, no.6 (1991): 1241–99.

Dacey-Groth, Camilla Elisabeth. *Representations of American Slavery in Post-civil Rights Fiction and Film: How Literature Shapes Politics*. Edwin Mellen Press, 2009.

Davis, Angela. "Reflections on the Black Woman's Role in the Community of Slaves." *The Black Scholar* 12, no. 6 (1981): 2–15.

Davis, Charles T. and Henry Louis Gates, Jr. *The Slave's Narrative*. Oxford UP, 1991.

Dawson, Lesel. "Revenge and the Family Romance in Tarantino's *Kill Bill*." *Mosaic: A Journal for the Interdisciplinary Study of Literature*, vol. 47, no. 2, 2014, pp. 121–134.

Django Unchained. Directed by Quentin Tarantino, performances by Jamie Foxx, Christoph Waltz, Leonardo DiCaprio, Kerry Washington, and Samuel L. Jackson, Weinstein Company/Anchor Bay, 2013.

Donaldson, Susan Van D'Elden. "Telling Forgotten Stories of Slavery in the Postmodern South." *The Southern Literary Journal*, vol. 40, no. 2, pp. 267–283.

Dunham, Jarrod. "The Subject Effaced: Identity and Race in Django Unchained." *Journal of Black Studies*, vol. 47, no. 5, pp. 402.

Eaton, Kalenda C. *Womanism, Literature, and the Transformation of the Black Community, 1965-1980.* Routledge, 2008.

Elliott, Missy. "Missy Elliott Lyrics—Work It." *AZ Lyrics.* Last modified January 3, 2015. www.azlyrics.com/lyrics/missymisdemeanorelliott/workit.html.

Fanon, Frantz. *Black Skin, White Masks.* New York: Grove Press, 2008.

Fleetwood, Nicole. *Troubling Vision: Performance, Visuality, and Blackness.* Chicago: U of Chicago P, 2011.

Forman, Murray. ""Movin' closer to an independent funk": Black Feminist Theory, Standpoint, and Women in Rap." *Women's Studies* 23, no. 1 (1994): 35–56.

Foster, William H. "Women Slave Owners Face Their Historians: Versions of Maternalism in Atlantic World Slavery." *Patterns of Prejudice*, vol. 41, no. 3–4, 2007, pp. 303–320.

George, Nelson. "An Essentially American Narrative: A Discussion of Steve McQueen's Film '*12 Years a Slave.*'" *The New York Times*, 11 Oct. 2013, p. AR18.

Giddings, Paula J. *When and Where I Enter: The Impact of Black Women on Race and Sex in America.* New York: W. Morrow, 1984.

Gilbert, Sandra M and Susan Gubar. *The Madwoman in the Attic: The Woman Writer and the Nineteenth-century Literary Imagination.* New Haven: Yale UP, 1984.

Gone with the Wind. Directed by Victor Fleming, George Cukor, Sam Wood, performances by Vivien Leigh, Clark Gable, and Leslie Howard, Loew's Inc., 1939.

Haley, Alex. *Roots: The Saga of an American Family.* Doubleday, 1976.

Haley, Alex and James Lee, creators. *Roots.* Wolper Productions, 1977.

Harris, Leslie. "*Ar'n't I a woman*, Gender and Slavery Studies." *Journal of Women's History*, vol. 19, no. 2, 2007, pp. 19–21.

Harris, Tamara Winfrey. "12 Years a Female Slave—Not Coming to a Theatre Near You." *The American Prospect*, 6 Nov. 2013. prospect.org/article/12-years-female-slave%E2%80%94not-coming-theatre-near-you

Harris, Trudier. *The Scary Mason-Dixon Line: African American Writers and the South.* Louisiana State UP, 2009.

Harris-Perry, Melissa. *Sister Citizen: Shame, Stereotypes, and Black Women in America.* 2nd ed. Yale UP, 2013.

Hartman, Saidiya V. *Scenes of Subjection: Terror, Slavery, and Self-Making in Nineteenth- Century America.* Oxford UP, 1997.

hooks, bell. *Feminism Is for Everybody: Passionate Politics.* South End Press, 2000.

Hopkinson, Natalie and Natalie Y. Moore. *Deconstructing Tyrone: A New Look at Black Masculinity in the Hip Hop Generation.* Cleis Press, 2008.

Hutcheon, Linda. "An Epilogue: Postmodern Parody: History, Subjectivity, and Ideology." *Quarterly Review of Film and Video*, vol. 12, no. 1–2, 1990, pp. 125–133.

Hutcheon, Linda. *A Poetics of Postmodernism: History, Theory, Fiction*. Routledge, 1988. "Iggy Azalea - D.R.U.G.S. ft. YG Lyrics HD." *YouTube*, uploaded by LOVE MUSIC, 2 Sept 2014, www.youtube.com/watch?v=hfMrDMFrEXw.

"Iggy Azalea Apologizes for Controversial 'Runaway Slave Master' Line." *Hip Hop DX*, 12 Mar 2012, hiphopdx.com/news/id.18983/title.iggy-azalea-apologizes-for -controversial-runaway-slave-master-line#

Jacobs, Harriet. *Incidents in the Life of a Slave Girl, Written by Herself*. New York: Penguin, 2000.

Jesser, Nancy. "Violence, Home, and Community in Toni Morrison's *Beloved*." *African American Review*, vol. 33, no. 2, 1999, pp. 325–345.

Jezebel. Directed by William Wyler, performances by Bette Davis, Henry Fonda, and George Brent, Warner Bros. Pictures, 1938.

Jones, Edward P. *The Known World*. Amistad, 2003.

Jones-Rogers, Stephanie. *They Were Her Property: White Women as Slave Owners in the American South*. https://yalebooks.yale.edu/book/9780300251838/ they-were-her-property/.

Kerman, Langston. A Barrel of Laughs, A Scattering of Slaves (with Michelle Buteau). https://www.iheart.com/podcast/1119-my-momma-told-me-with-lan-69919303/ episode/a-barrel-of-laughs-a-scattering-81171290/.

Kirlew, Shauna Morgan. "A Problematic Agency: The Power of Capital and a Burgeoning Black Middle Class in Edward P. Jones's *The Known World*." *South Atlantic Review*, vol. 79, no. 1–2, 2014.

Lackoff, George and Mark Johnson. *Metaphors We Live By*. U of Chicago P, 1980.

Lane, Nikki. "Black Women Queering the Mic: Missy Elliott Disturbing the Boundaries of Racialized Sexuality and Gender." *Journal of Homosexuality*, vol. 58, no. 6–7, 2011, pp. 775–792.

Leveen, Lois. "Dwelling in the House of Oppression: The Spatial, Racial, and Textual Dynamics of Harriet Wilson's Our Nig." *African American Review*, vol. 35, no. 4, 2001, pp. 561-580.

Lewis, Nghana. "Eaton, Kalenda C. *Womanism, Literature, and the Transformation of the Black Community, 1965–1980* and *Parodies of Ownership: Hip-Hop Aesthetics and Intellectual Property Law* (Book review)." *African American Review*, vol. 44, no. 1–2, pp. 291–96.

Li, Stephanie. "*12 Years a Slave* as a Neo-Slave Narrative." *American Literary History*, vol. 26, no. 2, 2014, pp.326–33.

Lorde, Audre. *Sister Outsider: Essays and Speeches*. Crossing Press, 1984.

Martin, Valerie. *Property*. Nan A. Talese, 2003.

McLarin, Kim. "Can Black Women and White Women Be True Friends?" *The Washington Post*. WP Company, March 29, 2019. www.washingtonpost.com/ nation/2019/03/29/can-black-women-white-women-be-true-friends/.

Miller-Young, Mireille. "Hip-Hop Honeys and Da Hustlaz: Black Sexualities in the New Hip- Hop Pornography." *Meridians: Feminism, Race, Transnationalism*, vol. 8, no. 1, 2008, pp. 261+.

Missy Elliott. "Missy Elliott—Work It (HQ)." Filmed [September 2002]. YouTube, 4:25. Posted [October 2009]. www.youtube.com/watch?v=cjIvu7e6Wq8..

Mitchell, Margaret. *Gone with the Wind*. Macmillan Publishers, 1936.

Morgan, Joan. *When Chickenheads Come Home to Roost: My Life as a Hip Hop Feminist*. Simon & Schuster, 1999.

Morrison, Toni. *Beloved*. Vintage, 2004.

Mukherjee, Roopali. "The Ghetto Fabulous Aesthetic in Contemporary Black Culture: Class and Consumption in the *Barbershop* Films." *Cultural Studies*, vol. 20, no.6, 2006, pp. 599-629.

Mullins, Katie L. "Black Female Identity and Challenges to Masculine Discourse in Rah Digga's *Dirty Harriet*." *Popular Music and Society*, vol. 36, no.4, 2013, pp. 425–443.

Ott, Brian L. ""I'm Bart Simpson, who the hell are you?" A Study in Postmodern Identity (Re)construction." *Journal of Popular Culture*, vol. 37, no.1, 2003, pp. 56–83.

Patterson, James Braxton. *The Hip-Hop Underground and African American Culture: Beneath the Surface*. New York: Palgrave Macmillan US, 2014.

Perry, Imani. "Who(se) Am I?: The Identity and Image of Women in Hip Hop." *Gender, Race, and Class in Media: A Text Reader*. 2nd edition. Eds. Gail Dines and Jean Humez. Thousand Oaks: Sage Publications, 2003. 136–148.

Pough, Gwendolyn. *Check It While I Wreck It: Black Womanhood, Hip-Hop Culture, and the Public Sphere*. Boston: Northeastern UP, 2004.

Pough, Gwendolyn, Elaine Richardson, Aisha Durham, and Rachel Raimist, eds. *Home Girls Make Some Noise!: Hip-hop Feminism Anthology*. Mira Loma: Parker Publishing, 2007.

Rah Digga. *Hip Online: Music Biographies, Reviews & Interviews*. Interview by Charlie Craine. WordPress, 2000. hiponline.com/2897/rah-digga-interview -2000.html.

Rah Digga. "Rah Digga Lyrics—Harriet Thugman." Genius Lyrics. Last modified June 7, 2015. genius.com/Rah-digga-harriet-thugman-lyrics.

Ralph, Michael. "Theoretical Ramifications of *Django Unchained*." *American Anthropologist*, vol. 117, no. 1, 2015, pp. 402–422.

Reed, Ishmael, editor. *Black Hollywood unChained: Commentary on the State of Black Hollywood*. Third World Press, 2015.

Reid-Pharr, Robert. *Kara Walker: Pictures From Another Time*. Edited by Annette Dixon, Thelma Golden, and Kara Walker. Ann Arbor, MI: University of Michigan Museum of Art, 2002.

Robertson, Claire and Marsha Robinson. "Re-modeling Slavery as If Women Mattered." *Women and Slavery, Vol 2: The Modern Atlantic*. Editors Gwyn Campbell, Suzanne Miers, and Joseph C. Miller. Ohio UP, 2007. 253–283.

Rose, Tricia. *Black Noise: Rap Music and Black Culture in Contemporary America*. Middletown: Wesleyan UP, 1994.

Rosen, Christopher. "Armond White's '12 Years A Slave' Review Compares Film to 'Human Centipede,' 'Hostel.'" *The Huffington Post*, 16 Oct 2013, www .huffingtonpost.com/2013/10/16/armond-white-12-years-a-slave_n_4110763.html, Accessed 3 Jul 2016.

Rushdy, Ashraf H. A. *Neo-Slave Narratives: Studies in the Social Logic of a Literary Form*. Oxford UP, 1999.

Schur, Richard L. *Parodies of Ownership: Hip-Hop Aesthetics and Intellectual Property Law*. U of Michigan P 2009.

Sellen, Eliza. "Missy 'Misdemeanor' Elliott: Rapping on the Frontiers of Female Identity." *Journal of International Women's Studies* 6, no.3 (2005): 50–63.

Sharpley-Whiting, T. Denean. *Pimps Up, Ho's Down: Hip Hop's Hold on Young Black Women*. NYU P, 2008.

Skillz. "Skillz Lyrics—The Rap Up 2012." *Genius*. genius.com/Skillz-2002-rap-up -lyrics

Smitherman, Geneva. ""The Chain Remain the Same": Communicative Practices in the Hip Hop Nation." *Journal of Black Studies* 28, no.1 (1997): 3–25.

Spaulding, A. Timothy. *Re-Forming the Past: History, The Fantastic, and the Postmodern Slave Narrative*. Ohio UP, 2005.

Speck, Oliver C. *Django Unchained: The Continuation of Metacinema*. Bloomsbury Academic, 2014.

Stallings, L.H. ""I'm Goin Pimp Whores!": The Goines Factor and the Theory of a Hip-Hop Neo-Slave Narrative." *CR: The New Centennial Review* 3, no.3 (2003): 175–203.

Stowe, Harriet Beecher. *Uncle Tom's Cabin*. Wordsworth Editions Ltd., 1999.

Swales, John. *Genre Analysis: English in Academic and Research Settings*. Cambridge UP, 1990.

Tademy, Lalita. *Cane River: A Novel*. Grand Central Publishing, 2001.

Thaggert, Miriam. "12 Years a Slave: Jasper's Look." *American Literary History*, vol. 26, no. 2, 2014, pp. 332–338.

Tucker, Lauren R. and Hemant Shah. "Race and the Transformation of Culture: The Making of the Television Miniseries *Roots*." *Critical Studies in Mass Communication*, vol. 9, no. 4, 1992, pp. 325–326.

Tweet. "Oops (Oh My) feat. Missy Elliott Lyrics." *AZ Lyrics*, www.azlyrics.com/ lyrics/tweet/oopsohmy.html.

12 Years a Slave. Directed by Steve McQueen, Performances by Chiwetel Ejiofor, Michael K. Williams, Michael Fassbender, and Lupita Nyong'o, Twentieth Century Fox, 2014.

Walker, Christine. *Jamaica Ladies: Female Slaveholders and the Creation of Britain's Atlantic Empire*. https://uncpress.org/book/9781469658797/jamaica-ladies/.

Wallace, Michele. "Uncle Tom's Cabin: Before and After the Jim Crow Era." *TDR: The Drama Review*, vol. 44, no. 1, 2000, pp. 137–156.

Wardi, Anissa Janine. "Freak Shows, Spectacles, and Carnivals: Reading Jonathan Demme's "Beloved."" *African American Review*, vol. 39, no. 4, 2005, pp. 513–526.

Wardle, Elizabeth and Doug Downs. *Writing about Writing: A College Reader*. Bedford/St. Martins, 2011.

West, Carolyn. "Mammy, Jezebel, Sapphire, and Their Homegirls: Developing an "Oppositional Gaze" Toward the Images of Black Women." *Lectures on the Psychology of Women.* 4th edition. Eds. Joan C. Chrisler, Carla Golden, and Patricia D. Rozee. New York: McGraw Hill, 2008. 286–299.

White, Deborah Gray. *Ar'n't I a Woman: Female Slaves in the Plantation South.* New York: W. W. Norton & Co, 1999.

Wood, Kirsten. "Broken Reeds and Competent Farmers: Slaveholding Widows in the Southeastern United States, 1783–1861." *Journal of Women's History,* vol. 13, no. 2, 2001. pp. 34–57.

Index

About the Author

Dr. Dana Horton is an assistant professor of English at Mercy College. Her areas of specialization include African American literature, Black women writers, hip hop studies, popular culture, feminist theory, slave narratives, and multiethnic literature. Dr. Horton's scholarly work has appeared in *Americana: The Journal of American Popular Culture*, *Lateral: Journal of the Cultural Studies Association*, and is forthcoming in *Global Hip Hop Studies*. She received her PhD in English at Northeastern University and her BA in English and African American studies at Temple University. In her free time, Dr. Horton enjoys riding her bike, playing volleyball, watching documentaries, and collecting purple items.

www.ingramcontent.com/pod-product-compliance
Lightning Source LLC
Chambersburg PA
CBHW022325280326
41932CB00010B/1234